Recipes
for a
HEALTHY
LIFESTYLE

by
Virginia Defendorf

**GOLDEN
WEST** ☼
PUBLISHERS

Consult your doctor . . .

This book is based on my experiences and those of my husband and on our studies of nutritional literature. It is not intended, nor should it be regarded, as medical advice. Before changing any diet, first consult your doctor.

Library of Congress Cataloging-in-Publication Data

Defendorf, Virginia

Recipes for a Healthy Lifestyle: recipes for after-your-bypass
    by Virginia Defendorf.
Includes index.
    1. Coronary heart disease—Diet therapy—Recipes.
    2. Aortic coronary bypass—Patients—Rehabilitation.
    3. Low cholesterol diet—Recipes. 4. Salt-free diet—Recipes.
    5. Sugar-free diet—Recipes. I. Title.

ISBN 0-914846-95-7

Cover Illustration by Kris Steele

Printed in the United States of America

4th printing © 1998

Golden West Publishers
4113 N. Longview Ave.
Phoenix, AZ 85014, USA
(602) 265-4392

Dedication

To my husband Ed
who helped me by sampling recipes

To my daughter Irene
who inspired me
through countless hours of preparation
and motivated me to write the book

To my son John who
always wanted me to open a bakery
because my
"Italian pastries are the ultimate"

and, to my son Jack
who can never get enough of my pizza.

Foreword

There are few things in medicine that are as rewarding as seeing patients become motivated to help share their treatment.

Ed Defendorf developed severe coronary artery disease a few years ago. He required a quadruple bypass of his coronary arteries. Since then he has worked hard to decrease his risk for progression of atherosclerosis. His blood pressure was controlled. His elevated serum lipids (cholesterol 284 and triglycerides 584) were significantly reduced on a proper diet (cholesterol 181 and triglycerides 157).

Virginia Defendorf has helped her husband Ed by designing a healthy diet. It is clear, by reviewing these recipes that eating good food is also compatible with eating food which is good for your heart.

Daniel L. Fortmann, M.D.
Cardiology and Internal Medicine
San Juan Capistrano, CA

Introduction

My reasons for writing *Recipes for a Healthy Lifestyle* are two-fold.

The primary reason—to keep my family healthy—was necessitated by the heart by-pass surgery of my husband. Following the operation came the learning experience of preparing foods to provide the body with nutrients that would maintain a healthy heart and arteries.

Watchwords in this task included: **no salt, no fat, no cholesterol** and **reduced sugar**.

My second reason for writing the book was to make these foods tasty. It has become an obsession with me to create delicious, appetizing, as well as healthful, meals.

As a home economist instructor, I worked with many nutritionists and spent countless hours in my classroom and kitchen preparing the recipes I have included in *Recipes for a Healthy Lifestyle.* Recipes were altered, eliminating or reducing the offending ingredients by the addition of herbs and other ingredients. I have won numerous national contests simply by substituting ingredients.

My husband can enjoy tempting meals without worrying whether his arteries will clog up again. I have also kept my weight and cholesterol stable.

While traveling, we take a small electric skillet along and avoid having to eat at fast-food or fancy restaurants. On a recent trip to Hawaii, we took along the recipes I was preparing for this book, and an electric skillet, can opener, small paring knife, two plastic dishes and eating utensils. On our return, we were happy to note that each of us had not gained an ounce. Gone are the days when "I smelled food and gained ten pounds!"

I urge you to read labels when marketing. Some of the listed ingredients indicate "no cholesterol." However, when an item includes hydrogenated oils, then the hydrogenation process has created saturated fat. One good point that I have found easy to follow in preparing foods for my husband is to reduce the saturated fat to ten percent or less of total calories. If your daily calorie intake is 2,000 calories, then your saturated fat intake should not be more than 200 calories.

Note that ALL FATS (saturated, unsaturated, polyunsaturated, and monounsaturated) contain nine calories per gram. Protein and carbohydrates, on the other hand, are four calories per gram. (1 gram = 1,000 milligrams)

Sometimes, when we reach for a quick snack, we have a tendency to grab a sandwich without realizing what we put in that sandwich, or what we eat with it. For example, chicken noodle soup with one-third less salt contains two grams of saturated fat. No-salt peanut butter contains 16 grams of saturated fat per tablespoon. A peanut butter sandwich will include almost your daily allowance of saturated fat, including the amount of fat in the bread you used.

I have found it a blessing, after being out all day, to come home to find our dinner ready to pop into the oven or microwave for a quick warming. One day every two weeks, I cook up a few meals and freeze them in portions. I even prepare pizza and store it, covered with aluminum foil, in the freezer. Bread can be made three or four loaves at a time. After slicing, it can be stored in convenient quantities and kept in the freezer. It can be used right from the freezer by toasting.

Recipes in *Recipes for a Healthy Lifestyle* are created to keep everyone's heart and body in good condition. Once you start using the recipes, you will agree that when you eat out you'll be able to taste the salt and fat in restaurant foods. And, once you start baking your own bread, you'll never want store-bought bread again.

Turn the pages, prepare the wholesome foods, and make your heart happy. Not only will you be eating healthful meals, but you'll find every bite delectable.

Contents

Tips to Help Lower Fat, Cholesterol and Calories

SUBSTITUTE

...skim milk, buttermilk or yogurt for whole milk and cream.

...plain, unflavored yogurt for sweet or sour cream, mayonnaise and fat in recipes. To prevent yogurt from separating during cooking, mix in one tablespoon cornstarch, continue stirring on medium heat until thickened, then add to foods, creams, etc.

...one cup of low or non-fat cottage cheese with one tablespoon skim milk and lemon juice for sour cream. For dessert sauces and custards, add one-half teaspoon vanilla extract per cup for full-bodied taste.

LOW-FAT, LOW-CALORIE WHIPPED TOPPING:

Beat two egg whites with one-half teaspoon cream of tartar. Fold in three tablespoons sugar and one-half cup skim milk ricotta cheese. Can be used as a low-calorie topping or filling.

LOW-FAT WHITE SAUCE:

Thin sauce: one cup skim milk, one tablespoon flour, one tablespoon diet margarine

Medium sauce: one cup skim milk, two tablespoons flour, two tablespoons diet margarine

Thick sauce: one cup skim milk, three tablespoons flour, three tablespoons diet margarine

CHEESE:

Low-fat cottage cheese, farmers cheese, hoop cheese, skim milk cheese, pot cheese, part skim milk ricotta cheese, diet and low-calorie cheese, and no-cholesterol cheese. Use small amounts of Parmesan and Romano cheese.

GOOD NEWS!

Many food manufacturers are making non-fat products available! Check your grocery store for non-fat dairy foods and non-fat poultry items.

Salads
and
Salad Dressings

Calico Cabbage Salad

♥ Yield: 6 servings

1 med. ONION
2 cups GREEN CABBAGE
(shredded and chilled)
2 cups RED CABBAGE
(shredded and chilled)
2 sm. APPLES
(sliced and chilled)

2 Tbsp. CANOLA OIL
1/4 cup VINEGAR
1 tsp. CELERY SEED
Dash of BLACK
PEPPER

Slice half of onion into rings and set aside for topping. Chop remaining half onion. In a large bowl, combine chilled cabbages with chopped onion. Arrange a row of chilled apple slices and onion slices on top.

In a small bottle or jar, mix oil, vinegar and celery seed. Shake well. Just before serving, pour oil mixture over cabbage and add a dash of black pepper.

Per serving

Calories 212	Saturated Fat ......23 gm
Cholesterol 0	Sodium ....7.5 mg

Chef's Salad

1/2 cup VINEGAR
2 tsp. CANOLA OIL
1 tsp. ONION JUICE
1/4 tsp. DRY MUSTARD
2 tsp. SUGAR
Dash of ground BLACK PEPPER

Combine all ingredients in a small jar or dressing decanter. Shake well and set aside for salad.

1/2 head LETTUCE (torn bite size)
1/2 cup SPINACH (torn bite size)
1/4 cup CARROTS (grated or shredded)
1/4 cup CELERY (chopped)
1/4 cup GREEN PEPPERS (chopped)
1/2 cup CANADIAN HAM (chopped)
1/2 cup low-sodium CHEESE (cubed)
1/2 cup each RADISHES, ONION, CAULIFLOWER
** (chopped)**

In a large bowl, combine all salad ingredients. Just before serving, toss with dressing, coating all greens well.

Per serving

Calories 186	Saturated Fat ..... 0.8 gm
Cholesterol .... 7.0 mg	Sodium .... 345.7 mg

Creamy Chicken Salad

♥ Yield: 3 servings

Dressing

1 med. ORANGE
1/2 cup non-fat, plain YOGURT
1 tsp. HONEY
1/2 tsp. toasted SESAME SEED

Grate orange peel to equal 1/2 teaspoon. Peel orange and section, squeezing one teaspoon juice. Set aside.

In a small bowl, combine orange peel, orange juice, yogurt, honey and sesame seed. Cover and chill in refrigerator for 30 minutes. Reserve dressing for salad.

Salad

1/2 cup GRAPES (seedless)
1 cup cooked CHICKEN BREAST (cubed)
1/4 cup WALNUTS, (chopped)
2 Tbsp. CELERY (sliced thin)
fresh SPINACH LEAVES (torn)

In a large bowl, toss together above reserved orange sections, grapes, chicken, walnuts and celery. Line platter with spinach leaves and spoon salad on top of leaves. Spoon one tablespoon of dressing over each serving.

If any dressing is left, cover and refrigerate for other salads.

Per serving

Calories 308	Saturated Fat ..... 2.0 gm
Cholesterol .... 27.6 mg	Sodium .... 58.6 mg

Fisherman's Salad

♥ Yield: 4 servings

1 head LETTUCE (broken in small pieces)
1/2 bunch Romaine LETTUCE (broken in small pieces)
1 stalk CELERY (sliced)
2 Tbsp. PIMENTO (chopped)
1/2 cup LOBSTER (cooked and chopped)
3 oz. SHRIMP (cooked, shelled and chopped)
2 cans (6 oz. each) flaked SALMON
3 oz. cooked CRABMEAT
1 Tbsp. light MAYONNAISE
1 Tbsp. light FRENCH DRESSING
1 TOMATO (cut in thin wedges)
12 GREEN OLIVES
CROUTONS (made from homemade bread)

In a large bowl, combine first eight ingredients. In a smaller bowl, combine mayonnaise and French dressing. Stir vigorously and pour over salad. Garnish with tomato wedges and olives. Top with croutons.

This salad makes an excellent dinner platter all by itself.

Note: To make croutons, toast a few slices of homemade bread and cut into cubes.

Per serving

Calories 166	Saturated Fat ..... 1.3 gm
Cholesterol .... 29.0 mg	Sodium .... 244 mg

French Shrimp Salad

♥ Yield: 6 servings

Salad

6 oz. SHRIMP (cooked, deveined and chilled)
2 oz. WALNUT HALVES
1 lg. APPLE (sliced thin)
2 sliced, hard-cooked EGGS (yolk removed)
1 can (4 oz.) MUSHROOMS (drained)
1 cup iceberg LETTUCE (shredded)

Arrange ingredients in a large salad bowl.

Dressing

1 Tbsp. CELERY (minced)
1 Tbsp. VINEGAR
1 Tbsp. MUSTARD
2 Tbsp. CANOLA OIL
1 Tbsp. diet MAYONNAISE
Pinch of CAYENNE PEPPER

Mix ingredients in blender. Pour over salad.

Per serving

Calories 156	Saturated Fat ..... 1.0 gm
Cholesterol .... 55.3 mg	Sodium .... 103.5 mg

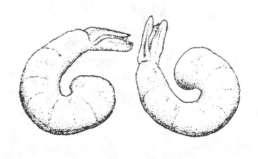

Vegetable Salad

♥ Yield: 6 servings

3/4 cup raw CARROTS (grated)
3/4 cup raw CAULIFLOWER (chopped)
1 can (8 oz.) PEAS (drained)
1/4 cup PIMENTO OLIVES (sliced)
3 Tbsp. OLIVE OIL
3 Tbsp. VINEGAR
3 Tbsp. CATSUP
1 tsp. SUGAR
Dash of BLACK PEPPER

In a medium-size salad bowl, combine first four ingredients. Combine remaining ingredients in a blender and whisk two seconds. Pour over vegetables one hour before serving.

Per serving

Calories 113.1	Saturated Fat ..... 0.9 gm
Cholesterol 0	Sodium .... 179.6 mg

Hawaiian Chicken Salad

♥ Yield: 4 servings

2 1/2 cups cooked CHICKEN BREAST
(skin removed, cut into
bite-size pieces)
3 Tbsp. CANOLA OIL
2 Tbsp. LEMON JUICE
1 can (14 oz.) crushed PINEAPPLE
(in own juice, drained)
1 cup CELERY (chopped)
5 Tbsp. diet MAYONNAISE
4 lg. LETTUCE LEAVES
1 oz. sliced ALMONDS

In shallow 8" pan, combine chicken with oil and lemon juice. Let marinate one hour. Transfer to a salad bowl with some of the marinade and add pineapple, celery and mayonnaise. Mix well.

Serve on bed of lettuce leaves and garnish with sliced almonds.

Per serving

Calories 262.5	Saturated Fat .....2.1 gm
Cholesterol ....25.7 mg	Sodium ....42.7 mg.

Seafood Pasta Salad

♥ Yield: 4 servings

1/4 cup non-fat, plain YOGURT
1/4 cup diet MAYONNAISE
2 Tbsp. ZESTY HERBS
2 Tbsp. PARMESAN CHEESE
2 cups CORKSCREW NOODLES (cooked and drained)
1 can (3 1/2 oz.) TUNA (water packed)
1 cup mixed, frozen VEGETABLES (defrosted)
1/2 cup GREEN PEPPER (chopped)
1/2 cup TOMATOES (chopped)
3 GREEN ONIONS (chopped)
4 LETTUCE LEAVES (optional)

Combine first three ingredients in medium-size salad bowl. Add remaining ingredients and mix well. Chill about 30 minutes.

Serve on lettuce leaves or as side dish.

Per serving

Calories 197	Saturated Fat ..... 1.0 gm
Cholesterol .... 10.0 mg	Sodium .... 179.7 mg

Three-Bean Salad

♥ Yield: 8 to 10 servings

2 cans (16 oz. each) GREEN BEANS (no salt, drained)
2 cans (16 oz. each) WAX BEANS (no salt, drained)
2 cans (15 1/4 oz. each) KIDNEY BEANS (drained)
1/2 cup GREEN PEPPER (chopped)
1/2 cup ONION (chopped)
2 sm. PIMENTOS (chopped)
1/2 cup CELERY (chopped)
1/2 cup VINEGAR
4 Tbsp. CANOLA OIL
1/2 tsp. BLACK PEPPER
1/2 cup FRUCTOSE
1/2 tsp. WORCESTERSHIRE SAUCE
1/2 tsp. CELERY SEED
Dash of GARLIC POWDER

In large bowl, mix first seven ingredients. Mix thoroughly. Add rest of ingredients and mix with hands, turning over vegetables to coat well. Cover with plastic wrap and refrigerate for 12 hours. Drain and serve as needed.

Salad will keep for several days in refrigerator.

Note: This salad can be served as a snack with crackers.

Per serving

Calories 165.7	Saturated Fat ..... 0.4 gm
Cholesterol 0	Sodium .... 181.0 mg

Creamy Salad Dressing

♥ Yield: 3/4 cup

1/2 cup BUTTERMILK
1 tsp. RED WINE VINEGAR (with garlic)
1 tsp. ONION FLAKES
Pinch BLACK PEPPER

Combine all ingredients and process in blender.

Per tablespoon serving

Calories 5.5	Saturated Fat ...0.06 gm
Cholesterol ....0.35 mg	Sodium ....10.7 mg

Coleslaw Dressing

♥ Yield: 3 cups

2 tsp. UNFLAVORED GELATIN
2 Tbsp. WATER
4 tsp. liquid ARTIFICIAL SWEETENER
1 tsp. dry MUSTARD
1/4 tsp. BLACK PEPPER
1/2 cup CIDER VINEGAR
1 Tbsp. ONION FLAKES
2 cups BUTTERMILK

Soften gelatin in water. Combine sweetener, mustard, pepper and gelatin in small saucepan. Stir and add vinegar. Heat to boiling. Stir until gelatin is melted. Add onion flakes and buttermilk. Mix well and store in refrigerator.

Per tablespoon serving

Calories 6.5	Saturated Fat ...0.05 gm
Cholesterol ....0.03 mg	Sodium ....11.2 mg

Mock Sour Cream

♥ Yield: 1/2 cup

1/4 tsp. WORCESTERSHIRE SAUCE
1 Tbsp. CIDER VINEGAR
2 Tbsp. WATER
1/2 cup low-fat COTTAGE CHEESE (non-fat preferred)
1/2 tsp. LEMON JUICE
3/4 tsp. chopped ONIONS (or CHIVES)

Place ingredients in blender and blend for two minutes or until smooth. Serve or refrigerate.

Per tablespoon serving

Calories	10.3	Saturated Fat	0.9 gm
Cholesterol	0.6 mg	Sodium	57 mg

Creamy Italian Dressing

♥ Yield: 3/4 cup

1/2 cup MOCK SOUR CREAM (see above)
1/4 tsp. BASIL
1/4 tsp. OREGANO
1/4 tsp. GARLIC POWDER
1/4 tsp. WORCESTERSHIRE SAUCE
1 Tbsp. CIDER VINEGAR
2 Tbsp. WATER

Place all ingredients in blender, blend at low speed for 30 seconds. Refrigerate and allow to clabber overnight for flavor.

Per tablespoon serving

Calories	7.5	Saturated Fat	0.06 gm
Cholesterol	0.04 mg	Sodium	39.8 mg

Creamy Cucumber Dressing

♥ Yield: 3/4 cup

1/2 cup MOCK SOUR CREAM (see page 19)
1/4 tsp. DILL
1/4 tsp. WORCESTERSHIRE
   SAUCE
1 1/2 Tbsp. chopped CUCUMBER
1 tsp. chopped ONION
1/4 tsp. CAPERS (drained)
1 1/2 tsp. WATER

Place ingredients in small container, blend thoroughly. Chill.

Per tablespoon serving

Calories 7.5	Saturated Fat ...0.06 gm
Cholesterol ....0.4 mg	Sodium ....40.0 mg

Russian Dressing

♥ Yield: 3/4 cup

1/2 cup MOCK SOUR CREAM (see page 19)
2 Tbsp. CHILI SAUCE
1/4 tsp. PAPRIKA
Dash of GARLIC POWDER
1 1/2 Tbsp. WATER

Place ingredients in small container, blend thoroughly. Chill.

Per tablespoon serving

Calories 10.6	Saturated Fat ...0.06 gm
Cholesterol ....0.04 mg	Sodium ....70.2 mg

French Dressing

♥ Yield: 1 cup

3/4 cup TOMATO JUICE
1 1/2 tsp. CATSUP
2 Tbsp. SAFFLOWER OIL
1 Tbsp. CIDER VINEGAR
1/2 tsp. prepared MUSTARD
1/4 tsp. CELERY SALT

Place all ingredients in blender, blend at low speed 30 seconds. Allow to clabber overnight for flavor.

Per tablespoon serving

Calories 18.9	Saturated Fat ..... 0.1 gm
Cholesterol 0	Sodium .... 78.4 mg

Sour Cream Dressing

♥ Yield: 1 cup

4 oz. FARMERS CHEESE
2 Tbsp. LEMON JUICE
1/2 cup BUTTERMILK

Mix all ingredients in blender. Good over both salads and vegetables.

Per tablespoon serving

Calories 7.5	Saturated Fat ... 0.02 gm
Cholesterol .... 0.06 mg	Sodium .... 1.18 mg

Pasta

Spinach Fettucini

♥ Yield: 6 servings

2 cups fresh SPINACH (finely chopped)
2 lg. EGG WHITES
1 Tbsp. CANOLA OIL
2 to 2 1/2 cups all-purpose FLOUR

Using food processor or mixer with dough hook, mix all ingredients. Start by adding only two cups of flour. Transfer to working board or area. Knead until smooth, using extra flour if too sticky. Let dough rest 10 minutes.

Separate in half, and roll out on working area horizontally to 18" x 18". Roll jelly roll fashion and, using a sharp knife, cut into three-eighth-inch rolls. Shake each roll down and place on flour-sprinkled towel. Let dry 30 minutes.

Fill 2-quart sauce pan three-fourths full with water and let come to boil. Drop in the fettucini and cook seven to ten minutes. (Should be slightly gummy.) Drain and serve with **Low-Cal Cream Sauce** on page 23.

Per serving

Calories 238		Saturated Fat .....1.1 gm	
Cholesterol 0		Sodium ....269 mg	

Low-Cal Cream Sauce

This is my favorite sauce, and is excellent with all of the recipes in this section.

♥ Yield: 3 3/4 cups

3 cups SKIM MILK
1/2 cup CREAM OF RICE cereal
1/2 cup PARMESAN CHEESE
2 Tbsp. BUTTER BUDS®

Using saucepan, heat milk. Do not boil! Add rest of ingredients. Stir and cook on low heat until thickened. Serve over fettucini. Will keep overnight in refrigerator. For smaller amounts, reduce ingredients by half.

Per tablespoon serving

Calories 8.5	Saturated Fat	0.1 gm
Cholesterol ....0.7 mg	Sodium	21.5 mg

Homemade Fettucini

♥ Yield: 4 servings

1 1/2 cups SEMOLINA FLOUR
1 Tbsp. OLIVE OIL
1 EGG WHITE (beaten frothy)
1/4 cup WATER (approximately)
1/2 cup all-purpose FLOUR

In a medium-size bowl, add semolina. Make a well and add oil, egg white and enough water to gather flour (while stirring) into a ball. If too sticky, add a little flour and knead about five minutes.

Cover and let rest 15 minutes. Divide dough into four parts. On clean surface, roll dough, one piece at a time, five inches wide and eight inches long. Sprinkle a little flour over dough and fold over (jelly roll fashion) from the short side. Cut with a very sharp knife into quarter-inch slices and shake, letting the fettucini unroll. Place on a flour-sprinkled towel and let dry 30 minutes to one hour.

Fill quart-size pan three-fourths full with cold water. Let come to a boil and drop in fettucini. Cook 8 to 10 minutes, stirring occasionally. Drain and place on platter. Serve with your favorite sauce, or use **Low-Cal Cream Sauce** on page 23.

Note: Semolina flour is found in most markets or health food stores. Also, if one is fortunate to own a pasta machine, use it by all means. This type of pasta can be frozen uncooked, wrapped in aluminum foil. It will keep up to six months.

Per serving

Calories 263	Saturated Fat ..... 0.5 gm
Cholesterol 0	Sodium .... 14.7 mg

Ukrainian Stuffed Dumplings

(Piroghi)

♥ Yield: 8 servings

DUMPLINGS

2 cups SEMOLINA FLOUR
1 EGG WHITE

1 Tbsp. CANOLA OIL
1/2 cup WATER

In medium-size bowl, place flour. Make a well and add egg white and oil. Add water and mix while gathering into a ball. If mixture appears too dry, add a little more water. Knead five minutes until dough becomes elastic. Let rest five minutes covered.

Roll dough out on flour-sprinkled pastry cloth or board. Cut into 3" x 3" squares and fill (recipe below). Fold over into triangles and seal edges with water and crimp.

Drop in 2-quart pan filled with boiling water, four or five at a time. Cook eight minutes. Lift with slotted spoon and place on platter. Serve with **Low-Cal Cream Sauce** (see page 23).

FILLING

4 boiled POTATOES (skinned and mashed)
1 cup PARMESAN CHEESE
1/4 cup minced PARSLEY
Sprinkle of BLACK PEPPER

In medium-size bowl, mix all ingredients well. Fill dumplings with one tablespoon each.

Per serving

Calories 236	Saturated Fat .....2.2 gm
Cholesterol ....8.0 mg	Sodium ....196.6 mg

Spinach Jumbo Pasta Shells

♥ Yield: 4 servings

4 Tbsp. diet MARGARINE
1 lb. cooked SPINACH (drained)
3/4 cup chopped ONIONS
1/2 cup PARMESAN CHEESE
1 cup RICOTTA CHEESE (low or non-fat)
1/4 tsp. NUTMEG
2 EGG WHITES (beaten frothy)
8 oz. JUMBO PASTA SHELLS
1 jar (16 oz.) homestyle SPAGHETTI SAUCE
1 cup LOW-CAL CREAM SAUCE*
Non-stick COOKING SPRAY (to spray skillet)

Preheat oven to 375 F. In sprayed 10" skillet, melt margarine and sauté spinach and onion. Add Parmesan and Ricotta cheese and nutmeg. Blend thoroughly. Add the beaten egg whites. Mix well and set aside.

Bring to boil a quart-size pan filled three-fourths full of water. Drop in pasta shells and cook six minutes. Drain shells thoroughly and fill with spinach mixture. Place in 10" x 10" baking dish. Heat spaghetti sauce in pan and spoon over shells alternating with spoonfuls of *Low-Cal Cream Sauce** (see page 23). Bake 25 minutes.

Per serving

Calories 539	Saturated Fat ..... 4.4 gm
Cholesterol .... 17.5 mg	Sodium .... 366.5 mg

Meatless Dishes

Basic Quiche Crust

♥ Yield: 10 servings

2 cups all-purpose FLOUR
2 tsp. BAKING POWDER

1/4 cup SKIM MILK
1/2 cup CANOLA OIL

Preheat oven to 400 F. In food processor or bowl, combine flour and baking powder. Mix milk and oil together and add to flour. Buzz until dough gathers into a ball. If mixing by hand, gather dough and form a ball.

Cover with plastic wrap and let rest 15 minutes. Separate dough into two equal parts. Sprinkle two pieces of wax paper with flour and place dough between sheets of wax paper. Starting from center, roll dough to size of quiche pan. Peel off top wax paper, fold dough in half and gently ease dough into pan, peeling bottom wax paper as you go along. Ease in with knuckles and, using a knife, cut along edges of pan. Dough should be even with edges of pan.

Per serving

Calories 193
Cholesterol ....0.1 mg

Saturated Fat .....1.4 gm
Sodium ....69 mg

Asparagus Quiche

♥ Yield: 6 servings

1 QUICHE CRUST*
10 stalks ASPARAGUS (cleaned and cut in halves)
1/2 lb. low-sodium SWISS CHEESE (diced)
2 Tbsp. PARMESAN CHEESE
6 EGG WHITES (beaten stiff)
3/4 cup (12 oz. can) SKIM EVAPORATED MILK
1 1/4 cups regular SKIM MILK

Preheat oven to 400 F. On bottom of quiche crust, place halved asparagus stalks evenly, adding Swiss and Parmesan cheese. In blender whisk together: egg whites, evaporated and skim milk. Blend for two seconds. Pour over asparagus mixture and bake in 400 F oven 35 to 40 minutes, or until inserted knife comes out dry. Serve hot or cold.

Note: Other vegetables such as broccoli, spinach, carrots and onions can be substituted. Adding a salad and/or fruit makes a delicious evening meal.

*See **Basic Quiche Crust** on page 27.

Per serving including crust

Calories	496.6	Saturated Fat	6.2 gm
Cholesterol	24.0 mg	Sodium	463.0 mg

Healthy Artichokes

♥ Yield: 2 servings

2 lg. ARTICHOKES
1 cup BREAD CRUMBS
2 Tbsp. OLIVE OIL
5 CLOVES GARLIC
WATER

Clean and cut off tips of artichokes. (Kitchen shears will make the job easier.) In small bowl, mix bread crumbs with olive oil and one clove garlic (pressed). Add enough water to make a thick paste. Divide into two portions. Spread artichoke leaves and fill with bread stuffing filling here and there, just enough to balance out.

Place artichokes in 2-quart pan filled with enough water to reach three-fourths up artichokes. Add rest of garlic cloves and cook, covered, on medium heat for one hour (or until a leaf pulls out easily). Serve hot or cold.

Note: To make bread crumbs, use four to eight slices of bread, toasted and whizzed in blender. If homemade bread is not available, other kinds will do.

It is not necessary to dip artichoke leaves in any dressing, as the stuffing flavors the leaves.

Per serving

Calories 333   Saturated Fat .....1.3 gm
Cholesterol 0   Sodium ....103. mg

Broccoli Omelet

♥ Yield: 2 servings

1 lg. stalk BROCCOLI (about 1/2 lb.)
1 pkg. (4 oz.) EGG SUBSTITUTE (found in dairy case)
Dash ground BLACK PEPPER
Dash SAVORY HERBS
Non-stick COOKING SPRAY (to spray skillet)

Wash and separate broccoli into flowerettes. Add water and broccoli to 1-quart saucepan and cook ten minutes or microwave on high for five minutes. Drain broccoli and chop.

In sprayed 10" skillet, add broccoli and toss until lightly crisp. Add rest of ingredients, cover and let cook until omelet is set and can be turned (about five to six minutes on medium heat).

Place a flat plate on top of omelet and turn skillet over onto plate. Slide omelet back in skillet and let brown about two minutes. Serve hot.

Note: This makes a delicious breakfast or light meal.

Per serving

Calories .... 85.2   Saturated Fat ..... 0.5 gm
Cholesterol 0   Sodium .... 70.2 mg

Easy Pizza

♥ Yield: 2 medium pizzas

4 cups all-purpose FLOUR
1 pkg. (1 Tbsp.) QUICK-RISING YEAST
1 2/3 cups warm WATER (warm to touch)
3 Tbsp. CANOLA OIL
Non-stick COOKING SPRAY (to spray pans)

Preheat oven to 400 F. Pour flour in a medium-size bowl. Make a well and add yeast, water and oil. Gather dough into a ball and keep on turning while kneading until smooth (about seven to ten minutes). Add a little flour if dough becomes sticky. Place dough in lightly-oiled bowl, cover and let rise for one hour.

Divide dough in half. Spray two 14" pizza pans. Pat dough into pans to edge, forming a lip. Add a little oil on top of dough (one tablespoon) and spread with hands evenly. Add toppings of choice and bake at 400 F for 20 to 25 minutes.

Note: To make this a low-calorie pizza, any vegetable topping can be used, such as zucchini, onions, tomatoes and tomato sauce with a low-fat cheese sprinkled on top.

Per serving

Calories 153.9	Saturated Fat ..... 0.2 gm
Cholesterol 0	Sodium .... 1.0 mg

Stir-Quick Pizza

♥ Yield: 4 servings

Pizza

2 cups all-purpose FLOUR
2 tsp. BAKING POWDER
2/3 cup SKIM MILK
1/4 cup CANOLA OIL
3 Tbsp. CANOLA OIL (for pan and drizzle)
Desired filling

Preheat oven to 425 F. In large bowl, measure flour and baking powder. (No need to sift.) Make a well, add milk and oil. Stir vigorously with a wooden spoon until mixture leaves side of bowl. Gather dough into a ball and knead 10 times. Cover and set aside for 15 minutes.

Sprinkle working area with flour and roll dough beginning at center, rolling outward until a circle is formed to fit 10-inch pan. Fold in half, lift and place in pizza pan. Ease dough in place, making a raised lip on edge to hold in filling.

Drizzle the three tablespoons oil on top and fill with desired filling. Bake at 425 F for 30 minutes.

Filling

Your choice of 1/2 cup amounts: Thinly-sliced **ONIONS, PEPPERONI, GREEN PEPPER, MUSHROOMS, TOMATOES**, low-sodium shredded **CHEESE, TOMATO SAUCE**. Add a sprinkle of **OREGANO**.

Per serving

Calories	454.5	Saturated Fat	2.3 gm
Cholesterol	0.7 mg	Sodium	1.8 mg

Italian Dried Tomatoes

♥ Yield: 6 servings

3 lbs. ripe PEAR TOMATOES
1 tsp. SALT SUBSTITUTE

Preheat oven to 200 F. Wash tomatoes and slice lengthwise. Lay them seed up on 10" x 18" baking sheet and sprinkle with salt substitute.

Bake at 200 F for five hours. (Check every hour to make sure one side cooks same as under side.) Tomatoes should shrivel up when done.

Cool and store in airtight container in freezer or use immediately. (See **Stuffed Dried Tomatoes** page 34.)

Per serving

Calories 48	Saturated Fat ..... 0.1 gm
Cholesterol 0	Sodium .... 20.3 mg

Stuffed Dried Tomatoes

♥ Yield: 6 servings

2 cups homemade BREAD CRUMBS
1 cup ONION (chopped)
1/2 tsp. BASIL (fresh or dried)
1/2 tsp. fresh PARSLEY (minced)
2 Tbsp. CANOLA OIL
1/2 cup TOMATO SAUCE (any brand will do)
BLACK PEPPER to taste
12 halves DRIED TOMATOES
Non-stick COOKING SPRAY (to spray pans)

Preheat oven to 350 F. In sprayed 10" skillet, sauté all ingredients except dried tomatoes. Sauté for five minutes while mixing thoroughly. Remove from heat and cool slightly.

Put one heaping tablespoon of stuffing in center of a dried tomato half and top with another half tomato. Place a toothpick through both halves and stuffing, and set in 9" casserole.

Bake at 350 F for 20 minutes.

Note: Can be used as a side dish or appetizer.

Per serving

Calories 288	Saturated Fat ..... 1.2 gm
Cholesterol 0	Sodium .... 171.1 mg

Stuffed Tomatoes with Corn Pudding

♥ Yield: 6 servings

6 firm, med.-size TOMATOES
1 EGG
1 Tbsp. FLOUR
1 tsp. SUGAR
1/4 tsp. BAKING POWDER
1/2 cup SKIM MILK
1 cup CORN KERNELS (canned or fresh)
1 Tbsp. diet MARGARINE (melted)
1 Tbsp. fresh PARSLEY (minced)
Sprinkle of PARMESAN CHEESE

Preheat oven to 350 F. Slice tops off tomatoes, scoop out pulp and seed (save pulp). Invert tomatoes on paper towel to drain.

In medium-size bowl, beat egg and add flour, sugar and baking powder. Blend in milk, and stir in corn and melted margarine. Thoroughly mix all ingredients, including pulp.

Spoon mixture into tomato shells and arrange in muffin tins. Bake at 350 F for 50 minutes (or until filling is puffed and browned). Garnish with parsley and cheese.

Per serving

Calories .... 91.5   Saturated Fat ..... 0.6 gm
Cholesterol .... 36.1 mg   Sodium .... 174 mg

Individual Spinach Pockets

♥ Yield: 6 servings

1 lb. fresh SPINACH (cooked and drained)
1 lb. RICOTTA CHEESE
1 lg. EGG
1 Tbsp. PARMESAN CHEESE
Dash of NUTMEG, GARLIC POWDER & BLACK PEPPER
1 pkg. (12 sheets) PHYLLO DOUGH (found in dairy case)
4 Tbsp. melted diet MARGARINE
1/2 cup CRACKER CRUMBS (use crumbled soda
   crackers)

Before preparing recipe, thaw phyllo dough according to instructions on package. Preheat oven to 350 F.

In medium-size bowl, add first four ingredients and spices. Mix well and set aside. Open thawed package of phyllo dough and lay flat on damp towel. Cover dough with another damp towel.

Separate two sheets of dough at a time, taking care not to tear sheets. Brush with melted margarine and sprinkle with one teaspoon cracker crumbs evenly. Fold in half. Place two tablespoons of spinach mixture in middle and fold over, forming an envelope. Each time you fold over, brush with melted margarine. Place pockets on baking sheet and pierce top with fork tines. Continue with other five pockets. Bake at 350 F for 35 minutes (or until browned).

Note: Spinach Pockets can be served with **Low-Cal Cream Sauce** (see page 23).

Per serving

Calories 271.5	Saturated Fat .....5.2 gm
Cholesterol ....71.6 mg	Sodium ....352.6 mg

Dilled Green Beans

1 pkg. (10 oz.) frozen, cut GREEN BEANS
2 GREEN ONIONS (finely chopped)
2 tsp. CORN STARCH
1/2 cup WATER
1/4 tsp. DILL WEED
1 tsp. CIDER VINEGAR
1 tsp. instant CHICKEN GRANULES
1/2 tsp. grated LEMON PEEL
Dash BLACK PEPPER

Place beans in steamer (or quart-size pan) with small amount of water. Cook on medium heat 10 minutes (or until tender). Drain and set aside.

Add rest of ingredients in another saucepan and cook on medium heat until sauce is slightly thickened. Pour over green beans and toss to coat. Serve hot or cold.

Per serving

Calories 20	Saturated Fat 0
Cholesterol 0	Sodium .... 10.5 mg

DILL

Italian Green Beans

♥ Yield: 4 servings

1 lb. GREEN BEANS
2 Tbsp. OLIVE OIL
2 Tbsp. GARLIC CLOVES (minced)
Ground BLACK PEPPER
Sprinkle of SAVORY HERBS

Stem and wash beans. Steam in steamer according to directions (or cook in microwave on high for 10 minutes, covered with plastic wrap).

When cooked to almost tender stage, place on large platter and add rest of ingredients. Toss lightly and serve hot.

Per serving

Calories 94	Saturated Fat .....0.6 gm
Cholesterol 0	Sodium ....277 mg

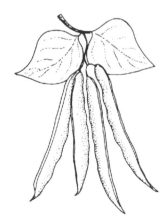

No-Meat Chili-Vegetable Dish

♥ Yield: 6 servings

1/4 cup CANOLA OIL
2 cups chopped ONION
2 cups EGGPLANT (with peel and chopped)
2 cups CELERY (chopped)
2 cups TOMATOES (peeled and chopped)
1 can (10 oz.) KIDNEY BEANS
2 tsp. CHILI POWDER (reduce to 1 tsp. if too spicy)
1 cup WATER
BLACK PEPPER (to taste)
Handful CROUTONS

Heat oil in 10" skillet and sauté onion until tender (about five minutes). Set aside. Combine rest of vegetables, including juice from kidney beans. Add chili powder and water, and season with pepper. Add the sautéed onion, including the drippings from skillet.

Cook in a covered 2-quart sauce pan on medium heat until eggplant is soft (about 30 minutes). Serve hot with croutons on top.

Note: A sprinkle of Parmesan cheese can be added on top for added flavor.

Per serving

Calories 177	Saturated Fat ..... 0.9 gm
Cholesterol 0	Sodium .... 213 mg

Nutritious Omelet

♥ Yield: 2 servings

1 Tbsp. CANOLA OIL
3 slices CANADIAN BACON (cut in 1/2-inch pieces)
1/2 lg. ONION (chopped)
1/2 GREEN PEPPER (chopped)
1/2 RED PEPPER (chopped)
1 pkg. (4 oz.) EGG SUBSTITUTE
1 tsp. fresh PARSLEY (minced)
Sprinkle of BLACK PEPPER

Heat oil in 10" skillet and sauté bacon, onion, green and red peppers. While bacon mixture is cooking, whisk egg substitute, pour over ingredients. Cover and let cook until omelet is dry on top (about three minutes).

Place a platter on top, remove skillet from heat and turn omelet over onto platter. Slide omelet back in skillet and cook one minute more. Serve hot. This makes a delicious breakfast or hearty lunch.

Per serving

Calories 156.5	Saturated Fat ..... 1.6 gm
Cholesterol .... 20.4 mg	Sodium .... 547 mg

Pancakes

♥ Yield: 4 servings

2 pkgs. (8 oz.) EGG
   SUBSTITUTE
1 cup SKIM MILK
1/2 cup WATER
2 1/2 cups FLOUR (sifted)

1 tsp. BAKING POWDER
2 Tbsp. CANOLA OIL
1 tsp. SUGAR
Non-stick COOKING SPRAY
   (to spray skillet)

Mix all ingredients thoroughly. Can use electric beater to mix lumps well. Pour into sprayed 10" skillet, three circles of batter at a time. When bubbles appear, turn over and cook until lightly browned. Serve immediately.

Note: Use low-calorie syrup or berries for topping. Do not spread with butter!

Per serving

Calories	432	Saturated Fat	1.2 gm
Cholesterol	1.0 mg	Sodium	164 mg

French Toast

♥ Yield: 2 servings

1 pkg. (4 oz.) EGG
   SUBSTITUTE
2 Tbsp. non-fat MILK

4 slices homemade BREAD
Non-stick COOKING SPRAY
   (to spray skillet)

Place egg substitute in medium-size bowl and add milk. Whisk until frothy. Dip bread in mixture, turning and making sure bread is well-coated. Place on sprayed 10" skillet and brown both sides on medium heat.

Per serving

Calories	204	Saturated Fat	0.8 gm
Cholesterol	1.7 mg	Sodium	311 mg

Poultry

Baked Oat Bran-Coated Chicken

♥ Yield: 2 servings

1 cup OAT BRAN
1 tsp. SAVORY HERBS
1 tsp. ITALIAN HERBS
2 CHICKEN BREASTS
  (skinned and cleaned)

3 Tbsp. plain, NON-FAT
  YOGURT
BLACK PEPPER
Non-stick COOKING SPRAY
  (to spray baking dish)

Preheat oven to 400 F. Mix together in a medium-size brown paper bag: oat bran, savory herbs and Italian herbs. Using clean hands, coat chicken breasts with yogurt. Drop into paper bag containing oat bran mixture and shake to coat all sides.

Place in prepared 10" x 13" baking dish. Sprinkle with black pepper. Bake at 400 F, 45 to 55 minutes, turning so each side is browned.

Per serving

Calories	325	Saturated Fat	0.8 gm
Cholesterol	73.3 mg	Sodium	21.8 mg

Chicken Casserole with Broccoli & Cheese

**3 CHICKEN BREASTS, cooked and cut into 2" pieces
(can use part dark meat)**
**2 pkgs. (12 oz. each) frozen BROCCOLI (cooked
and drained)**
2 cans (10 1/2 oz. each) CREAM OF CHICKEN SOUP
1/4 cup lite MAYONNAISE
1 Tbsp. LEMON JUICE
3 shakes LEMON PEPPER
1 1/2 cups shredded CHEDDAR CHEESE

Preheat oven to 350 F. Layer 10" x 10" baking dish with cut-up pieces of chicken. Add cooked broccoli on top. Mix soup, mayonnaise and lemon juice. Spread over top. Add lemon pepper and spread the cheddar cheese on top of all ingredients. Bake at 350 F for 30 minutes.

Per serving

Calories 270	Saturated Fat .....7.5 gm
Cholesterol ....72.6 mg	Sodium ....661 mg

Moo Goo Gai Pan

(Chicken in the Pan)

♥ Yield: 10 servings

2 Tbsp. CANOLA OIL
3 slices GINGER ROOT (minced)
2 CLOVES GARLIC
4 CHICKEN BREASTS (skinned and cut into 2" pieces)
2 CELERY ribs (cut diagonally into 1/2" pieces)
1/4 cup (2 oz.) BAMBOO SHOOTS
8 WATER CHESTNUTS (sliced in halves)
5 oz. fresh MUSHROOMS (cooked and drained)
2 Tbsp. SOY SAUCE
2 tsp. SHERRY
2 Tbsp. CORNSTARCH (or arrowroot) dissolved
      in 1/2 cup CHICKEN BROTH

Mix first three ingredients in 10" skillet. Sauté three minutes and remove garlic and ginger. Add chicken, stir fry until pieces turn white and then remove.

Add celery, bamboo shoots, water chestnuts and mushrooms. Stir fry one minute. Add soy sauce, sherry and cornstarch mixture. Mix well and add chicken. Cook on medium heat until sauce bubbles (about 15 minutes). Serve over/or with rice.

Per serving

Calories 139	Saturated Fat ..... 0.9 gm
Cholesterol .... 29.2 mg	Sodium .... 112.7 mg

Crisp Chicken Breasts

♥ Yield: 4 servings

4 CHICKEN BREAST halves
4 CHICKEN LEGS
2 tsp. HERB BLEND
1 tsp. PAPRIKA
1/2 tsp. PEPPER
1 cup FLOUR
4 EGG WHITES (beaten frothy)
2 Tbsp. NON-FAT MILK
1/4 tsp. MUSTARD
3 cups fine BREAD CRUMBS (homemade if possible)
1 tsp. fresh PARSLEY
Non-stick COOKING SPRAY (to spray baking pan)

Preheat oven to 425 F. Remove skin from chicken. Wash each piece and drain. Combine herbs, paprika, pepper and flour. In separate dish, combine egg whites, milk and mustard. Again, in a separate dish, combine bread crumbs with parsley.

Dip chicken pieces in flour mixture, then in egg mixture and finally in bread crumb mixture. Coat evenly and place in shallow, sprayed, baking pan.

Refrigerate 10 minutes. Bake 10 minutes at 425 F, then reduce heat to 375 F and bake an additional 30 minutes. Serve with a hearty green salad and fruit dessert.

Per serving

Calories 408.4	Saturated Fat ..... 0.7 gm
Cholesterol ..... 114.1 mg	Sodium .... 245.6 mg

Good-for-Your-Heart Chili

♥ Yield: 4 to 5 servings

1 Tbsp. OLIVE OIL
1 lg. ONION, chopped
1 lb. GROUND TURKEY (light and dark meat)
2 cans (32 oz. each) KIDNEY BEANS
    (low salt if possible)
1 can (16 oz.) STEWED TOMATOES (low salt)
1 Tbsp. CHILI POWDER (or to taste)
1 Tbsp. Hungarian PAPRIKA
10 oz. WATER

Using a two-quart pan, add olive oil and onion. Sauté two minutes on medium heat. Add turkey. Sauté until turkey is all opaque. Add rest of ingredients. Stir thoroughly.

Cook over medium heat for 45 minutes to one hour, stirring occasionally. Serve with homemade croutons or low-salt crackers.

Note: Chili can be divided in portions and frozen for later use.

Per serving

Calories 375	Saturated Fat ... 0.09 gm
Cholesterol .... 68.6 mg	Sodium .... 708.4 mg

Sweet and Sour Kabobs

♥ Yield: 4 to 5 servings

**1 can (16 oz.) PINEAPPLE CHUNKS (in own juice)
    (drain and save juice)**
1/4 cup RED WINE VINEGAR
1 Tbsp. CANOLA OIL
2 drops SOY SAUCE
1 1/4 tsp. CORNSTARCH
1 pkg. artificial SWEETENER
1/2 tsp. granulated GARLIC
1 lb. TURKEY BREASTS (cut into 1" pieces)
**2 med. CARROTS (sliced into 1" pieces and cooked
    five minutes)**
1 lg. GREEN PEPPER (cut into 1" or 2" pieces)
1 lg. RED PEPPER (cut into 1" or 2" pieces)
1 lg. YELLOW PEPPER (cut into 1" or 2" pieces)

Combine pineapple juice, vinegar, oil, soy sauce, cornstarch, sweetener and garlic in 1-quart saucepan. Cook, stirring until thickened. Set aside.

Thread pineapple chunks, turkey, green pepper, turkey, red pepper, turkey, yellow pepper, and turkey on four long skewers. (Alternate pieces until all is used.) Brush with above sauce and broil or barbeque 12 to 18 minutes, brushing with sauce one or two more times.

Turn kabobs, brush again and continue cooking five minutes more. Serve hot.

Note: This dish can be served with brown rice or spinach noodles.

Per serving

Calories	240	Saturated Fat	1.2 gm
Cholesterol	62.6 mg	Sodium	76.4 mg

Sweet and Sour Turkey

♥ Yield: 4 servings

2 1/2 cups cooked TURKEY (skinned and cubed)
1 med. ONION (thinly sliced)
1/4 cup chopped GREEN PEPPER
1 lg. chopped CELERY STALK
1 pkg. (10 oz.) frozen PEA PODS
1 can (16 oz.) PINEAPPLE CHUNKS (in own juice)
1 tsp. instant CHICKEN BOUILLON granules
1 tsp. powdered GINGER
1 tsp. BROWN SUGAR
1 1/2 tsp. SOY SAUCE (low sodium)
1 Tbsp. APPLE CIDER
4 tsp. CORNSTARCH
2 Tbsp. WATER

Combine first five ingredients in a wok or 10" skillet. Stir fry until turkey is well browned (about seven minutes). Add rest of ingredients and stir well. Keep stirring until all ingredients are heated through and broth is slightly thickened.

Serve with **Sweet and Sour Sauce** on page 49.

Per serving

Calories 288	Saturated Fat .....1.2 gm
Cholesterol ....66.2 mg	Sodium ....204. mg

Sweet and Sour Sauce

♥ Yield: 4 servings

1/2 cup unsweetened PINEAPPLE JUICE
5 Tbsp. CATSUP
2 tsp. white APPLE CIDER
1/2 cup WATER
1 tsp. minced ONION
3 drops TABASCO® SAUCE

Combine all ingredients in 1-quart pan. Bring to a boil on medium heat and let bubble three minutes. Serve over turkey or other favorite foods.

Per serving

Calories	39	Saturated Fat	0.01 gm
Cholesterol	0	Sodium	221 mg

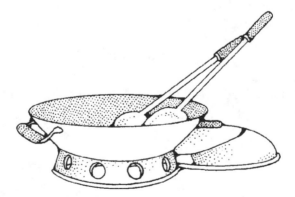

Turkey Burgers

♥ Yield: 2 servings

1/2 lb. ground TURKEY (no skin)
1/2 cup OAT BRAN
1 EGG WHITE
1/2 cup minced ONION
1 Tbsp. fresh, chopped PARSLEY
1 tsp. ground BASIL
1/2 tsp. SAVORY HERBS
1/2 tsp. ground BLACK PEPPER
Non-stick COOKING SPRAY (to spray skillet)

In medium-size bowl, mix all of the ingredients in order. Form into two large patties on aluminum foil and refrigerate for 15 minutes.

Spray 10" skillet and add patties. Brown on both sides. If skillet dries too fast from heat, add one tablespoon canola oil and cook 15 to 20 minutes on medium-low heat.

Per serving

Calories	311	Saturated Fat	1.9 gm
Cholesterol	86. mg	Sodium	110 mg

Turkey Eggplant Parmesan

♥ Yield: 4 to 5 servings

1 med.-size EGGPLANT
1 lg. ONION, sliced thin
1 lb. ground TURKEY (97 percent fat-free at least)
1 jar (28 oz.) homestyle SPAGHETTI SAUCE (no-salt)
1 Tbsp. dried BASIL
1/2 cup BREAD CRUMBS (homemade if possible)
8 oz. shredded CHEDDAR CHEESE (no cholesterol)
2 Tbsp. grated PARMESAN CHEESE
Ground BLACK PEPPER
Non-stick COOKING SPRAY (to spray skillet)

Peel eggplant and slice into 1/2" circles. Using a sprayed 10" skillet, brown eggplant on both sides. To brown evenly, spray each slice of eggplant. Set aside.

In same skillet, sauté onion until opaque. Add turkey, continue to sauté until cooked and slightly browned (15 to 20 minutes).

Pour a little spaghetti sauce on the bottom of sprayed 10" casserole. Arrange in layers: eggplant, turkey mixture, spaghetti sauce, basil, a sprinkle of bread crumbs, and half the cheddar cheese. Make two layers, ending with half of the cheddar cheese. Top with the Parmesan cheese and pepper.

Microwave covered with plastic film for 15 minutes on medium setting.

Per serving

Calories	328.4	Saturated Fat	4.9 gm
Cholesterol	30.8 mg	Sodium	29.7 mg

Filled Turkey Rolls

♥ Yield: 5 to 6 servings

1 lb. ground TURKEY (can use light and dark meat)
1 cup ITALIAN BREAD CRUMBS (see note)
1 CLOVE GARLIC (minced)
1 sm. ONION (chopped)
1/4 cup PARSLEY (minced)
2 EGG WHITES (slightly beaten)
1/4 cup WATER
Non-stick COOKING SPRAY (for baking dish)

Mix all above ingredients in a medium bowl. Set aside.

Filling

1 can (16 oz.) TOMATOES (no salt)
2 slices low-calorie CHEDDAR CHEESE
1 sm. ONION (thinly sliced)
5 to 6 BAY LEAVES

Preheat oven to 400 F. Drain tomatoes (reserve juice) and chop coarsely. Slice cheese into 10 to 12 strips. Divide filling ingredients into five or six portions.

At this point, also divide turkey mixture (above) into five or six portions. Place one portion of turkey mixture on palm of one hand and pat into a pattie as large as the hand.

With free hand, place in center of pattie one portion each tomato, cheese and onion. Roll over the pattie by bending the fingers in a cupping motion, encasing the filling in the pattie and seal by pressing

(Continued on next page)

(Continued from previous page)

at both ends with other hand. Rolls should be about as large as your fist.

Place turkey rolls in sprayed 10" x 10" baking dish and top each roll with a bay leaf. Pour reserved juice on top and bake at 400 F for 45 minutes (or until rolls are dark roasted). Add more tomato juice if needed or rolls appear too dry. Discard bay leaves.

Serve warm or cold.

Note: For Italian bread crumbs, use four to five slices of bread, toasted and whizzed in blender.

Per serving

Calories	264	Saturated Fat	3.4 gm
Cholesterol	68.0 mg	Sodium	494 mg

Turkey Meatballs
with Tomato Sauce

♥ Yield: 4 servings

1 lb. ground TURKEY BREAST (skin removed)
1 cup BREAD CRUMBS (preferably homemade)
1/2 cup chopped fresh PARSLEY
1 tsp. dried BASIL
2 GARLIC CLOVES (pressed)
1/2 tsp. BLACK PEPPER
2 EGG WHITES (beaten frothy)
2 tsp. PARMESAN CHEESE
4 oz. WATER (approximately)
1 jar (28 oz.) TOMATO SAUCE (no salt)
Non-stick COOKING SPRAY (to spray skillet)

In a large bowl combine all ingredients except tomato sauce. Mix well. If mixture appears too dry, add a little more water. Roll into walnut-size balls. In prepared 10" skillet, add turkey balls and brown on all sides. Set aside.

In a 1-quart pan, pour tomato sauce, adding one-half jar of water. Mix thoroughly. Bring to a simmer, add turkey balls. Let simmer for 45 minutes.

Serve over pasta dishes.

Note: Shrimp may be used in place of turkey. Simply boil shrimp until they turn pink.   Shell, devein, and add to sauce. Simmer 45 minutes.

Per serving
Calories 290
Cholesterol .... 80.0 mg
Saturated Fat ..... 1.8 gm
Sodium .... 193.7 mg

Turkey Sausage

♥ Yield: 4 to 5 servings

1 lb. ground TURKEY (no skin)
1 cup BREAD CRUMBS
1/2 cup fresh PARSLEY (chopped)
1 tsp. dried BASIL
2 GARLIC CLOVES (minced)
Dash BLACK PEPPER
2 EGG WHITES (beaten frothy)
2 tsp. PARMESAN (or Romano) CHEESE
4 oz. WATER (approximately)
1/2 cup FENNEL SEEDS
1/2 cup RED WINE
Non-stick COOKING SPRAY (to spray skillet)

In a large bowl, mix all ingredients. If mixture appears too dry, add a little more wine. Divide mixture into four or five portions. Again divide each portion into three, and roll into a sausage roll. Continue until all portions are divided and rolled.

In sprayed 10" skillet, brown sausages on all sides. Cook over medium heat until well-cooked (about 15 minutes).

Serve with fettucini or any vegetable dish.

Per serving

Calories 167.8	Saturated Fat ..... 1.2 gm
Cholesterol .... 27.0 mg	Sodium .... 127.6 mg

Turkey Pot Pies
(low fat)

♥ ♥ Yield: 3 servings

1 lb. TURKEY BREAST (no skin)
Enough WATER to cover turkey
1 Tbsp. PICKLING SPICES
1/4 cup RICE FLOUR
1 pkg. (10 oz.) frozen VEGETABLES
2 Tbsp. BUTTER FLAVORING
Ground BLACK PEPPER

Preheat oven to 400 F. In a quart-size pan, add enough water to cover turkey. Then add pickling spices. Cook on top of stove for about one hour (or until tender). Remove turkey from broth and cut into bite-size pieces. Set aside.

Strain turkey broth into a clean quart-size pan, and add rice flour. Cook on low heat until slightly thickened. Add cut-up turkey, frozen vegetables and butter flavoring. Mix well. If too thick, add a little water. Add pepper. Set aside.

Top Crust

1 1/2 cups WHEAT FLOUR
4 Tbsp. diet MARGARINE
6 to 7 tsp. ICE WATER

In medium-size bowl, mix together flour and margarine. Work with fork tines until margarine becomes incorporated with flour. Add water and with fork tines gather into a ball. Divide into three pieces

(Continued on next page)

(Continued from previous page)

and refrigerate.

Fill ramekins (can use baking dishes) with turkey mixture right to top. Roll out cold dough and fit over each ramekin. Slit center of crust with a sharp knife. Brush top with any leftover diet margarine. Continue with the other two ramekins. Set pot pies on a foil-covered baking sheet and bake at 400 F for 45 minutes. Serve hot.

Per serving

Calories 325.6	Saturated Fat ..... 1.9 gm
Cholesterol .... 62.6 mg	Sodium .... 169.6 mg

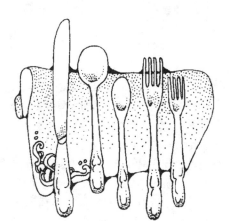

Seafoods

Broiled Halibut

♥ Yield: 2 servings

1 tsp. PAPRIKA
1 Tbsp. OLIVE OIL
2 HALIBUT fillets (1/2" thick)

Ground BLACK PEPPER
LEMON slices

Combine paprika and olive oil. Place halibut fillets on aluminum foil and brush both sides with the paprika mixture. Sprinkle with ground pepper. Broil two inches under broiler. Brush again with paprika mixture and turn. Broil each side about five minutes.

Serve immediately with lemon slices on top.

Per serving

Calories 102
Cholesterol .... 35.0 mg

Saturated Fat ..... 1.3 gm
Sodium .... 59 mg

Broiled Ahi
(Yellow Fin Tuna)

♥ Yield: 3 servings

1 lb. YELLOW FIN TUNA
1 Tbsp. CANOLA OIL
1/2 tsp. PAPRIKA
Non-stick COOKING SPRAY (to spray pans)
2 LEMONS (use juice)
6 CARROTS
1 lg. ZUCCHINI
1 Tbsp. OLIVE OIL
Ground PEPPER (to taste)

Clean fish and discard all outer dark skin. Mix canola oil with paprika and brush over fish. Place fish in sprayed 9" x 10" baking dish. Broil five minutes on each side. (Can be done on barbecue grill.)

Squeeze lemon juice while fish is broiling. Slices of lemon can be added on top, also.

Peel carrots and zucchini, julienne both and stir fry with olive oil in 8" skillet. Cook five to eight minutes. Serve with fish.

Note: The flesh of ahi is very dark and the flavor excellent.

Per serving

Calories 358	Saturated Fat ..... 1.2 gm
Cholesterol .... 63.3 mg	Sodium .... 61.6 mg

Broiled Swordfish

♥ Yield: 5 servings

2 lbs. SWORDFISH
2 Tbsp. SOY SAUCE (low sodium)
1 CLOVE GARLIC (minced)
2 Tbsp. LEMON JUICE
1/2 tsp. ground GINGER
1/2 tsp. artificial SWEETENER

Cut fish into 1 1/2-inch cubes and place in a bowl. Combine the rest of ingredients and pour over fish. Cover and refrigerate at least six hours. Baste about three times while it is in refrigerator.

Place fish in 10" x 10" baking dish and broil four inches from heat for 10 minutes, turning pieces to brown on all sides. Baste with remaining marinade during broiling.

Per serving

Calories 113	Saturated Fat ..... 2.8 gm
Cholesterol .... 33.6 mg	Sodium .... 377 mg

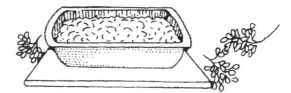

Italian Halibut

Yield: 2 servings

2 slices fresh or frozen HALIBUT (1/2-inch thick)
2 Tbsp. OLIVE OIL
3 lg. GARLIC CLOVES (sliced thin)
1 can (16 oz.) stewed TOMATOES (no salt)
BLACK PEPPER
SAVORY HERBS
1/2 cup all-purpose FLOUR
Non-stick COOKING SPRAY (to spray skillet)

Clean fish and discard all bones. Set aside. Put oil and garlic in 8" skillet and sauté slowly until garlic is light brown. Slowly add stewed tomatoes and a dash of pepper and herbs. Simmer 20 to 30 minutes.

While tomato mixture is cooking, flour fish on both sides and place in another sprayed 8" skillet. Spray a little cooking spray on top of fish and brown on both sides. Lower heat and sauté 30 minutes, turning about two times. If fish is too dry, add a little more spray on bottom of skillet. Fish must be crisp. When fish flakes (test a corner with fork), remove to platter.

Add tomato mixture on top of each piece. Serve hot.

Per serving

Calories 459	Saturated Fat ..... 3.4 gm
Cholesterol .... 35.0 mg	Sodium .... 61.0 mg

Crabmeat Waldorf

♥ Yield: 1 serving

1 Tbsp. LEMON JUICE
1 red APPLE (unpeeled
   and diced)
2 oz. CRABMEAT* (flaked)
1 Tbsp. PICKLE (chopped)
1 Tbsp. PIMENTO (chopped)
1/4 cup CELERY (or cucumber,
   chopped)
1 Tbsp. WALNUTS (chopped)

Sprinkle lemon juice on apple. In small bowl, combine and toss all ingredients. Chill and serve on bed of lettuce.

Note: Can also add thawed, frozen peas and sliced radishes.

*To reduce sodium run crab under cold water.

Per serving

Calories 104.2	Saturated Fat ..... 0.2 gm
Cholesterol .... 23.2 mg	Sodium .... 612.0 mg

Old-Fashioned Fish Soup

♥ Yield: 4 servings

3 CLOVES GARLIC (peeled and sliced)
2 Tbsp. OLIVE OIL
1 Tbsp. PARSLEY FLAKES
1 can (16 oz.) stewed TOMATOES (no salt)
1 lb. WHITE FISH fillets
4 cups WATER
1 cup ABC NOODLES (or rosamarina, or anci di peppe)
Ground PEPPER and extra PARSLEY

Place garlic with oil in 2-quart saucepan and sauté for two minutes. Add parsley and tomatoes. Cook down, stirring until slightly reduced (about 10 minutes).

Add fish fillets and simmer until fish flakes (about 20 minutes).

Add noodles to four cups of water boiling in another 2-quart saucepan. Cook until tender (or al dente).

Drain and add to tomato-fish mixture. Simmer five minutes more. Serve immediately with dash of pepper and parsley.

Note: Rosamarina, anci di peppe or ABC noodles are a barley-type pasta available where other pasta products are sold.

Per serving

Calories 213	Saturated Fat .....2.3 gm
Cholesterol ....25.4 mg	Sodium ....256 mg

Poached Salmon

3 cups WATER
2 slices SALMON fillets (half-inch thick)
1/2 ONION (sliced)
1 Tbsp. PARSLEY
1 Tbsp. BUTTER BUDS®
1/2 cup white WINE
Ground BLACK PEPPER (sprinkle)
1 LEMON (sliced)

In a shallow 10" pan (such as a skillet), add ingredients in order. Top salmon with lemon slices. Let poach on medium heat, covered, about five to seven minutes. Lift fish carefully out of water with a spatula and place on warm plate. Add more lemon and pepper. Serve hot with a sprinkle of parsley (optional).

Per serving

Calories 238		Saturated Fat .....1.6 gm
Cholesterol ....74.1 mg		Sodium ....146 mg

Salmon in a Pouch

♥ Yield: 2 servings

2 slices SALMON fillets (3/4-inch thick)
1 Tbsp. OLIVE OIL
1 tsp. PAPRIKA
Dash BLACK PEPPER
Dash GARLIC POWDER
1 LEMON (sliced)
Non-stick COOKING SPRAY (use for spray coating)

Preheat oven to 425 F. Clean and remove all visible bones from salmon. Curl ends to form a round fillet with each slice. Mix oil, paprika, pepper and garlic thoroughly. Brush on both sides of fish and wrap fish in sprayed parchment or aluminum foil, forming an envelope. (Make sure pouch ends are folded over enough so juices will not escape.)

Place in 8" x 8" casserole and bake at 425 F for 25 minutes. Open pouches and serve immediately with slices of lemon on top of fish.

Note: This fish can be served right out of the pouch.

Per serving

Calories 255	Saturated Fat ..... 2.6 gm
Cholesterol .... 74.1 mg	Sodium .... 57.1 mg

Red Snapper

♥ Yield: 4 servings

1/4 tsp. TARRAGON
1/2 tsp. PARSLEY FLAKES
1/2 tsp. BLACK PEPPER
1/2 tsp. minced ONION
1 lb. RED SNAPPER fillets
6 to 8 slices LEMON
Non-stick COOKING SPRAY (to spray casserole)

Preheat oven to 400 F. Combine first four ingredients. Arrange fish in prepared 8" x 8" casserole. Sprinkle with seasoning mixture. Top each fillet with lemon. Bake at 400 F for 10 to 15 minutes, or until fish flakes easily with a fork.

Note: This is a fast dish and can be prepared easily when one comes home from work. Scrumptious without effort!

Per serving

Calories 146	Saturated Fat ..... 0.4 gm
Cholesterol .... 53.2 mg	Sodium .... 64.1 mg

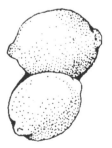

Seafood Kabobs

♥ Yield: 4 servings

1 lg. GREEN PEPPER (cut in 1" pieces)
1 lb. SCALLOPS (cut in halves, try large size)
1/2 lg. ONION (cut in wedges)
4 CHERRY TOMATOES
2 Tbsp. SOY SAUCE (low salt)
1 Tbsp. LEMON JUICE
1/4 tsp. PAPRIKA
1/4 tsp. GARLIC POWDER

On each skewer (use four 8" or 9" long skewers), alternate green pepper, scallop and onion with a cherry tomato in center. Continue until skewers are all filled evenly.

In a small bowl, combine soy sauce, lemon juice, paprika and garlic powder to form sauce. Place filled skewers on roasting rack under broiler and brush with sauce mixture.

Broil 15 minutes, until scallops appear opaque and green pepper is tender. Take out and brush skewered items with sauce again, all around. Finish broiling another 10 minutes. Serve immediately.

Note: Place a tray under broiler to catch drippings.

Per serving

Calories 125.7	Saturated Fat ..... 0.4 gm
Cholesterol .... 4.7 mg	Sodium .... 704 mg

Shrimp and Scallops on a Skewer

♥ Yield: 4 servings

1/2 lb. SHRIMP (shelled and deveined)
1/2 lb. SCALLOPS (use whole)
1 lg. GREEN PEPPER (cut in 8 pieces)
1 lg. ONION (cut in 8 pieces)
1 lg. TOMATO (cut in 8 pieces)
8 lg. MUSHROOMS
1 Tbsp. PAPRIKA
1 Tbsp. OLIVE OIL
Ground BLACK PEPPER
CAJUN HERBS
4 Tbsp. LEMON JUICE

Alternate first six ingredients on skewers (four 8" or 9" long) in order given.

In a small bowl, combine next four ingredients and brush over filled skewers. Place skewers on roasting rack under broiler and broil five minutes.

Take out and add lemon juice over each skewer. Return to broiler for five to eight minutes more, turning to cook evenly. Serve hot on a bed of rice or with vegetables of choice.

Note: Place a tray under broiler to catch drippings.

Per serving

Calories 141.5	Saturated Fat .....0.6 gm
Cholesterol ....86.9 mg	Sodium ....148.4 mg

Tuna a la King

♥ Yield: 1 serving

1 can (3 oz.) MUSHROOMS
1/2 cup SKIM MILK
1/2 tsp. PARSLEY FLAKES
Dash BLACK PEPPER
1 can (6 oz.) TUNA (water packed, drained)
1 slice BREAD (toasted)

Drain mushrooms and place in a blender. Add milk, parsley and black pepper. Pureé one to two seconds. Pour into 1 quart saucepan and add tuna. Heat to almost boiling. Spoon over toast.

Note: Mushroom sauce can also be used over vegetables.

Per serving

Calories 347	Saturated Fat ..... 0.6 gm
Cholesterol .... 2.0 mg	Sodium .... 769 mg

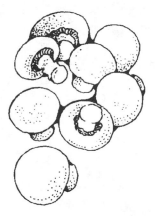

Tuna Casserole

♥ Yield: 4 servings

1 can (12 oz.) TUNA (water-packed)
1 lb. corkscrew PASTA or bows (cooked and drained)
1 Tbsp. PARSLEY (minced fresh or dried)
4 oz. non-fat plain YOGURT
4 Tbsp. diet MARGARINE
1 Tbsp. PARMESAN CHEESE
1 sm. ONION (minced)
1 cup BREAD CRUMBS (for topping)
Non-stick COOKING SPRAY (to spray casserole)

Preheat oven to 400 F. In a large bowl, mix all ingredients except bread crumbs. Use half of water in can of tuna. Mix thoroughly and pour into prepared 10" x 10" casserole. Top with bread crumbs.

Bake at 400 F for 20 minutes. This dish can also be prepared in microwave on high about 10 minutes. (If using microwave, cover with plastic film.)

Note: To make bread crumbs, use four to six slices of homemade bread, toasted and whizzed in blender. Other breads can be used if homemade is not available.

Per serving

Calories 247.5	Saturated Fat ..... 0.6 gm
Cholesterol .... 21 mg	Sodium .... 132.7 mg

Breads

Batter White Bread

♥ Yield: 2 loaves
(12 slices each)

2 pkgs. (1/4 oz. each) ACTIVE DRY YEAST
2 3/4 cups WARM WATER (95-100 degrees)
6 1/2 cups all-purpose FLOUR
3 Tbsp. SUGAR
2 Tbsp. soft MARGARINE (melted)

Preheat oven to 375 F. In bowl of electric mixer, sprinkle yeast into the warm water. Let stand two minutes, then stir until dissolved. Add 3 1/4 cups flour, sugar and melted margarine. Blend at low speed, then beat two minutes at medium speed. Beat in remaining flour, using a spoon. Cover and let rise until double (about 45 minutes).

Stir batter, beating hard. Spread in two greased 9" x 5" pans. Let rise in pans until double again (about 20 minutes). Bake at 375 F for 40 to 50 minutes.

Each slice

Calories 114	Saturated Fat ...0.03 gm
Cholesterol 0	Sodium ....9.4 mg

Chewy Bread Sticks

♥ Yield: 128 bread sticks

1 pkg. (1/4 oz.) YEAST (rapid-rising)
1 1/2 cups WARM WATER (110-degree temp.)
1 Tbsp. HONEY
5 cups FLOUR
Non-stick COOKING SPRAY (to spray baking sheet)

Preheat oven to 400 F. In electric mixer, dissolve yeast in warm water. Add honey and gradually add flour. Mix until mixture pulls away from bowl. Place on a floured board or surface and knead by hand until dough can be handled. Spray a little cooking spray on top and continue kneading.

Cut with sharp knife into 32 pieces. Then cut each piece into four pieces. Roll these four pieces into 12-inch ropes each. Arrange on sprayed 10" x 10" baking sheet one-inch apart. Continue with rest. (Having more than one baking sheet makes the job easier.) Let rise in warm place covered, until puffy.

Bake at 400 F for 20 minutes. Bread sticks can be frozen after baking, and when needed, thawed and rebaked for five minutes at 300 F.

Each bread stick

Calories 18.6	Saturated Fat 0
Cholesterol 0	Sodium .... 0.1 mg

Cheesy Onion Health Loaves

♥ Yield: 2 round loaves
(12 slices per loaf)

5 2/3 cups all-purpose FLOUR
1 cup WARM WATER (90 degrees)
2 pkgs. (1/4 oz. each) DRY YEAST (rapid-rising)
2 tsp. BAKING POWDER
1 cup ONION (minced)
2 Tbsp. CARAWAY SEEDS
2 cups COTTAGE CHEESE (low or non-fat)
1 EGG YOLK (mix with 1 Tbsp. water for glaze)

Preheat oven to 350 F. In a small bowl, measure 2/3 cup unsifted flour. Add water and yeast. Let sit for five minutes.

Add remaining flour in a large bowl with baking powder, onion and caraway seeds. Mix with a wooden spoon and stir in the cottage cheese. Keep stirring and add yeast mixture. Dough will be sticky.

With a handful of extra flour, work the dough in the bowl until handling becomes easy and kneading can be done (about four minutes). Knead until elastic, then form into two round loaves.

Set on 10" x 13" baking sheet sprinkled with cornmeal. Brush on egg yolk mixture. Let rise until double, or about 45 minutes, in a warm place with wax paper cover. Bake at 350 F for 50 to 60 minutes.

Each slice

Calories 128	Saturated Fat ..... 0.2 gm
Cholesterol .... 9.6 mg	Sodium .... 105 mg

Manitoba Bread or Rolls

♥ Yield: 2 loaves or 24 rolls

2 1/2 cups lukewarm WATER (to touch)
1 Tbsp. SUGAR
2 pkgs. (1/4 oz. each) YEAST (rapid-rising)
6 cups BREAD FLOUR
1 pkg. (4 oz.) EGG SUBSTITUTE
1 tsp. SALT
3 oz. CANOLA OIL
EGG YOLK (mix with 1 Tbsp. water for glaze)

Preheat oven to 400 F. In a small bowl, add water, sugar and yeast with one cup flour. Stir and set aside.

In a large bowl, add rest of flour, egg substitute, salt and oil. With a wooden spoon make a well and add the yeast mixture. Mix well and, using hands, gather dough and knead on flour-sprinkled working area. If dough is sticky, add a little flour and continue kneading until bouncy.

Place in a large oiled bowl, cover and let rise until double (about one hour). Punch down twice.

Shape risen dough into two round loaves, brush with egg-yolk glaze and bake in two 5" x 9" loaf pans for 50 minutes. For rolls, set side-by-side on 10" x 13" baking sheet. Brush with glaze and bake at 400 F for 30 minutes.

Each roll

Calories 146		Saturated Fat ..... 0.4 gm	
Cholesterol .... 8.8 mg		Sodium 94.0	

Mixer French Bread

♥ Yield: three 18" baguettes
(Nine 2" slices per loaf)

1 1/2 pkgs. (1/4 oz. each) YEAST (rapid-rising)
1/4 cup WARM WATER (95-100 degrees)
2 cups all-purpose FLOUR
1 1/4 cups COOL WATER
8 ICE CUBES
Non-stick COOKING SPRAY

Preheat oven to 425 F. In bowl of electric mixer, add yeast and warm water. Run mixer on low, so that yeast is completely dissolved. Add flour and mix on low two seconds more. Gradually add cool water and mix until batter forms into a large ball.

Sprinkle some flour on working area and knead dough by hand for 10 minutes. Spray a large bowl with cooking spray and place dough in it. Cover and let rise until double (one hour).

When dough is ready, place on working area and shape into three 18-inch baguettes (long tubulars). Place on prepared 10" x 13" baking sheet sprinkled with cornmeal and let rise about half volume. Score risen baguettes diagonally with razor blade, making four incisions about half-inch deep.

Bake at 425 F for 30 minutes. Throw ice cubes on floor of oven, two times during baking, to produce steam for crisp crust. Cool on metal rack.

Each slice

Calories 35	Saturated Fat ... 0.01 mg
Cholesterol 0	Sodium .... 1.1 mg

Sourdough Starter

♥ 2-quart size glass jar
(about 8 cups)

1 cup SKIM MILK
3 Tbsp. plain YOGURT
1 cup FLOUR
1/2 tsp. SUGAR

Heat milk to warm (not boiling). Remove from heat, stir in yogurt and flour with sugar. Stir well and pour into clean glass jar. Cover with plastic wrap and let stand 24 hours.

After 24 hours, stir the liquid that has come to surface and let stand in warm area, covered, two to five days, stirring occasionally. If pinkish liquid appears on top, discard liquid only, stir and let set covered in refrigerator until ready to use.

Note: Each time starter is used for bread making, replace with an equal amount taken out. (If one cup is used, replace as follows, 1/2 cup milk and 1/2 cup flour, stir and add to glass jar in refrigerator).

When needed again, bring to room temperature and continue. Also packages of sourdough starter can be found in health food stores and can be used as directed on package. Sourdough starter can be used over and over again when replenished and kept in refrigerator.

Each cup

Calories 66.7	Saturated Fat ...0.05 gm
Cholesterol ....0.3 mg	Sodium ....18.0 mg

Sourdough French Bread

♥ Yield: 2 large loaves
(12 slices each loaf)

2 pkgs. (1/4 oz. each) YEAST (rapid-rising)
1 1/2 cups WARM WATER (110 degrees)
1 cup SOURDOUGH STARTER
6 cups (approx.) all-purpose FLOUR
3 Tbsp. CARAWAY SEEDS
Non-stick COOKING SPRAY
2 Tbsp. CORN MEAL

Preheat oven to 400 F. Using a large bowl, dissolve yeast in warm water. Add sourdough starter and five cups of flour with the caraway seeds. If dough becomes too dry to handle, add a little extra warm water. Mix thoroughly, turning dough in kneading fashion. Cover and let rise to double (one hour).

When ready, place dough on floured working area and knead until elastic. Cut in half and roll into loaves. Place each half in a 5" x 8" bread pan coated with cooking spray and sprinkled with a tablespoon of cornmeal. Bake at 400 F for 40 minutes. Take out of pans and return to oven for five minutes more. Cool bread before slicing.

Note: If a more pronounced sour taste is desired, use two cups sourdough starter. Experiment with different seeds, such as sesame, dill and anise.

Each slice

Calories 118	Saturated Fat .. 0.05 gm
Cholesterol 0	Sodium .... 1.0 mg

Great Double All-Bran Muffins

♥ Yield: 18 muffins

3 cups whole BRAN CEREAL
1 cup BOILING WATER
2 EGG WHITES (beaten frothy)
2 cups BUTTERMILK
1/2 cup CANOLA OIL
1 cup RAISINS
2 1/2 cups all-purpose FLOUR
2 1/2 tsp. BAKING SODA
SUGAR SUBSTITUTE (to equal 1 cup of granulated
sugar)
1/2 cup WALNUTS (chopped)

Preheat oven to 425 F. In a large bowl, mix bran cereal with water. Stir completely to moisten. Set aside to cool.

When ready, add rest of ingredients, folding over to blend together. Stir well and refrigerate one hour (or overnight). Spoon into three 6-muffin tins lined with paper cups. Bake at 425 F for 25 minutes.

Note: If a smaller amount is needed, bake only amount needed and refrigerate batter. Batter will keep two weeks in refrigerator.

Each muffin

Calories 211	Saturated Fat .....0.9 gm
Cholesterol ....0.9 mg	Sodium ....243 mg

Desserts

Basic White Cake

♥ Yield: 15 to 20 servings

2 cups all-purpose FLOUR
1 1/2 Tbsp. BAKING
   POWDER (low sodium)
1 cup SUGAR
1/2 cup CANOLA OIL
1 cup SKIM MILK

1 tsp. VANILLA EXTRACT
4 EGG WHITES, plus 1/4
   cup SUGAR
Non-stick COOKING
   SPRAY (to spray pans)

Preheat oven to 350 F. Stir first three ingredients in bowl of electric mixer. Add oil, milk, and vanilla. Beat at high speed for two minutes.

In separate clean bowl, beat egg whites, adding the quarter-cup sugar. Beat until stiff. Fold into batter, folding over 10 times.

Pour into two round 8" cake pans sprayed and flour-coated. Bake at 350 F for 25 to 30 minutes.

Remove from oven and cool five minutes. Turn over onto serving tray and top with favorite fruit.

Per serving

Calories 150	Saturated Fat ..... 0.5 gm
Cholesterol .... 0.2 mg	Sodium .... 91.4 mg

Apple Cake

♥ Yield: 10 servings

1 cup whole wheat PASTRY FLOUR
1/4 cup FRUCTOSE
1 tsp. CINNAMON
3 Tbsp. diet MARGARINE (chilled)
1/2 tsp. BAKING SODA
1/2 cup BUTTERMILK
3 Tbsp. EGG SUBSTITUTE (found in dairy section)
3 med. APPLES (peeled and finely chopped)
1/4 cup WALNUTS (chopped)
3/4 cup non-fat YOGURT
Non-stick COOKING SPRAY (to spray baking pan)

Preheat oven to 375 F. In a large bowl, combine flour, fructose and cinnamon. Cut in margarine until mixture is crumbly. Remove 1/3 cup and set aside. Stir baking soda into remaining crumbs. Add buttermilk and egg substitute.

Mix well and add apples and yogurt. Blend thoroughly.

Turn into 9" round prepared cake pan. Mix reserved 1/3 cup crumb mixture with walnuts and sprinkle on top.

Bake at 375 F for 30 minutes. Cool and cut into wedges.

Per serving

Calories 123	Saturated Fat ..... 6.2 gm
Cholesterol .... 7.3 mg	Sodium .... 86.9 mg

Healthy Carrot Cake

♥ Yield: 25 two-inch pieces

4 EGG WHITES
1 tsp. CINNAMON
1 tsp. ALLSPICE
1/2 cup CANOLA OIL
1 can (7 1/2 oz.) crushed PINEAPPLE (in own juice)
2 cups FLOUR
1 tsp. BAKING SODA (use low sodium)
4 cups CARROTS (grated)
**SUGAR SUBSTITUTE (to equal 1 1/2 cups of
    granulated sugar)**
1 cup WALNUTS (coarsely chopped)
1 cup CONFECTIONERS SUGAR
**Non-stick COOKING SPRAY (to spray pan and wax
    paper).**

Preheat oven to 350 F. In electric mixer bowl, beat egg whites until frothy and add next four ingredients.

Mix flour with baking soda and add to mixture. If mixture is too dry, add a little water (about one-quarter cup). Fold in carrots, sugar substitute and walnuts. At this point, mix thoroughly.

Pour into 10" x 10" square pan lined with wax paper and sprayed. Bake at 350 F for 30 minutes. Cake will be moist. Let cool 15 minutes and turn out on platter or rack.

Peel off wax paper. When cake is completely cooled, sprinkle with confectioners sugar.

Per serving

Calories 82.7		Saturated Fat ..... 0.4 gm	
Cholesterol .... 0.07 mg		Sodium .... 76.4 mg	

Famous Fruitcake

♥ Yield: 2 cakes
(10 slices each cake)

1 pkg. (4 oz.) EGG SUBSTITUTE
1/2 cup BROWN SUGAR
2 lbs. mixed GLAZED FRUIT
1 lb. mixed NUTS (walnuts, brazil, hickory
     or almonds—chopped)
1 cup all-purpose FLOUR
1/4 tsp. BAKING SODA
1 tsp. BAKING POWDER
1/2 cup BRANDY
Non-stick COOKING SPRAY (to spray loaf pans)

Preheat oven to 280 F. In a large bowl, beat egg substitute with sugar. Set aside. In another bowl, combine next five ingredients, coating fruit and nuts thoroughly. Add to egg mixture. Add brandy and continue mixing until all ingredients are well blended.

Pour into two 5" x 8" loaf pans sprayed and lightly floured. Smooth out batter to corners with back of spoon. Bake at 280 F for 90 minutes. Remove cake from pans and turn on rack to cool.

Glaze

1/2 cup light SYRUP
1 Tbsp. WATER

Boil syrup and water in small pan. Brush on fruit cakes while syrup is hot. Decorate with some leftover glazed fruit. Let dry.

Each slice

Calories 205	Saturated Fat ..... 1.8 gm
Cholesterol 0	Sodium .... 28.7 mg

Quick & Easy Fruitcake

♥ Yield: 20 servings

3 cups self-rising FLOUR
1 jar (28 oz.) MINCEMEAT (no beef suet)
4 EGG WHITES
1/3 cup SKIM MILK
3 Tbsp. CANOLA OIL
2 cups mixed CANDIED FRUIT (reserve 1/4 cup
**   for decoration)**
1 cup WALNUTS (coarsely chopped)
1/4 cup light CORN SYRUP
1 Tbsp. WATER
1/2 cup BRANDY
Non-stick COOKING SPRAY (to spray pan)

Preheat oven to 325 F. In a large bowl, combine first seven ingredients. Turn and mix well with a wooden spoon. Spoon into a sprayed and floured 10" bundt pan, and even out smoothly.

Bake at 325 F for 75 minutes. Remove from oven and cool. Turn over on tray or leave in bundt pan.

In a small pan, bring syrup and water to a boil. Remove from heat, cool slightly and add brandy. Brush over cool cake, making sure to reach all of cake. Garnish with reserved candied fruit.

Can be sliced and wrapped individually in plastic wrap and frozen. Will keep indefinitely.

Per serving

Calories 167	Saturated Fat ...... 1.6 gm
Cholesterol 0	Sodium .... 83 mg

Candied Fruitcake

♥ Yield: 4 small cakes
(10 slices each cake)

**3 1/2 lbs. candied and glazed FRUIT (reserve some
for decoration)**
2 lbs. PECAN HALVES (reserve some for decoration)
2 cups all-purpose FLOUR
2 tsp. double-acting BAKING POWDER (low sodium)
1/2 cup COCOA
**SUGAR SUBSTITUTE (to equal 1/2 cup of granulated
sugar)**
1 pkg. (4 oz.) EGG SUBSTITUTE (found in dairy section)
4 Tbsp. non-fat plain YOGURT
1 tsp. MACE
4 sm. pieces CHEESECLOTH, for dipping
1/2 cup RUM
1/2 cup light CORN SYRUP
Non-stick COOKING SPRAY (to spray small pans)

Preheat oven to 325 F. In a large bowl, using your hands, mix all ingredients except rum and corn syrup. Turn over many times to make sure ingredients are mixed thoroughly.

Fill four 3" x 5" sprayed pans with batter mixture, making sure pans are filled to corners. Bake at 325 F for 50 minutes. Remove cakes from pans and let cool.

Dip cheesecloth in half cup rum and wrap around cakes. Cover with foil and refrigerate three to four days to soak in flavor. Boil corn syrup and brush over cakes. Decorate with glazed fruits and nuts.

Each slice

Calories	196	Saturated Fat	1.3 gm
Cholesterol	0	Sodium	17.8 mg

Easy Sour Cream Coffeecake

♥ Yield: 10 - 15 servings

1/2 cup diet MARGARINE
SUGAR SUBSTITUTE (to equal 3/4 cup of granulated
**   sugar)**
1 tsp. VANILLA EXTRACT
4 EGG WHITES
2 cups sifted FLOUR
1 tsp. BAKING POWDER (low sodium)
1 tsp. BAKING SODA (low sodium)
6 oz. plain non-fat YOGURT
Non-stick COOKING SPRAY (to coat pan)

Preheat oven to 350 F. In large bowl, mix margarine, sugar substitute and vanilla. Mix thoroughly. Add whites (one at a time) beating well after each addition.

Combine flour with baking powder and soda. Add to creamed batter, alternating with yogurt. Blend well. Spread half of batter in sprayed and floured 10" tube pan and layer with filling.

Filling

6 Tbsp. diet MARGARINE
2 tsp. CINNAMON
1 cup chopped WALNUTS
SUGAR SUBSTITUTE (to equal 1 cup of granulated
**   sugar)**
2 tsp. NUTMEG
1 cup APPLES (chopped)

Cream all ingredients except apples in a medium

(Continued on next page)

(Continued from previous page)

sized bowl. Fold in apples, coating well, and spread over cake batter. Cover with remaining batter and sprinkle with topping (see following).

Topping

1/2 cup WALNUTS (chopped)
1/2 cup BROWN SUGAR

Mix walnuts and sugar together, and sprinkle on top of cake.

Bake at 350 F for 50 minutes. While still warm, drizzle with glaze.

Glaze

1/2 cup CONFECTIONERS SUGAR
2 Tbsp. diet MARGARINE
2 Tbsp. SKIM MILK (warmed)

In small bowl, mix all ingredients with a fork. Continue mixing until thick enough to drizzle on cake.

Per serving

Calories	364.60	Saturated Fat	2.7 gm
Cholesterol	0.35 mg	Sodium	324.8 mg

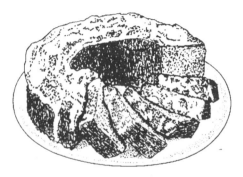

No-Eggs Vanilla Cake

♥ Yield: 9 servings

1 3/4 cups whole wheat PASTRY FLOUR
1 tsp. BAKING POWDER
1 tsp. LECITHIN granules (found in health food stores)
3/4 cup MAPLE SYRUP
1/3 cup CANOLA OIL
2/3 cup WATER
2 tsp. VANILLA EXTRACT
1 Tbsp. APPLE CIDER VINEGAR
Non-stick COOKING SPRAY (to spray baking pan)

Preheat oven to 375 F. In a large bowl, sift together flour, baking powder and lecithin granules. Pour in syrup, oil, water, vanilla and vinegar. Beat vigorously with wooden spoon, making sure no lumps remain.

Pour into sprayed and floured 9" square pan. Bake at 375 F for 30 to 40 minutes. Cool cake and remove from pan. Sprinkle powdered sugar on top (optional) or serve with sliced bananas.

Per serving

Calories	218	Saturated Fat	0.8 gm
Cholesterol	0	Sodium	40.3 mg

Low-Calorie, Low-Fat Crust

(for pies, tarts, turnovers and quiches)

♥ Yield: One 9" or 10" crust

1 cup all-purpose FLOUR
1/4 tsp. BAKING POWDER
3 Tbsp. diet MARGARINE (or regular tub margarine)
1/4 cup SKIM MILK

Preheat oven to 400 F. In a medium-size bowl, sift flour with baking powder. Add margarine and cut in with fork. Add milk and stir into a ball. Do not overhandle. Roll dough on flour-sprinkled area (or pastry cloth) and place in 9" or 10" pie pan. Crimp edges.

For pre-baked crust, pierce with fork tines before baking at 400 F for 20 minutes, covering edges with foil. For filled pies, do not pierce. Follow procedure in recipe and bake accordingly.

Note: For double crust pies, double amounts of ingredients above. This crust can be used for tarts and turnovers as well as quiche and pot pies.

Per serving

Calories 69.7	Saturated Fat ..... 0.3 gm
Cholesterol .... 0.1 mg	Sodium .... 58.2 mg

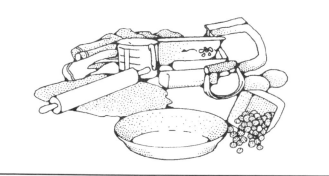

Flaky Pastry

♥ Yield: One 9" or 10" crust

1 1/2 cups all-purpose FLOUR
1/2 cup diet MARGARINE (very cold)
1 lg. EGG WHITE
2 tsp. LEMON JUICE
2 to 3 Tbsp. ICE WATER (or little more)
extra FLOUR to roll crust

Preheat oven to 425 F. Place all ingredients in food processor. Blend just enough to gather dough into a ball. If mixture seems too dry, add a little more water. Wrap in plastic wrap and chill in refrigerator for 30 minutes. Roll out on flour-sprinkled board to fit 9" or 10" pie pan. Cut and crimp edges.

Pierce with fork tines and bake at 425 F for 10 to 20 minutes. This crust can also be used for tarts or shells.

Per serving

Calories 128	Saturated Fat ..... 1.0 gm
Cholesterol 0	Sodium .... 127.5 mg

Lemon Filling

♥ Yield: Enough to fill one pie
or 8 custard servings

3/4 cup SUGAR
3 Tbsp. CORNSTARCH
1/8 tsp. SALT
3/4 cup WATER
1 tsp. grated LEMON PEEL
1/3 cup LEMON JUICE
1 Tbsp. MARGARINE
4 drops yellow FOOD COLORING

In quart-size saucepan, mix sugar, cornstarch and salt, stirring while adding the water. Cook over medium heat, stirring constantly until mixture thickens. Boil one minute and remove from heat.

Add lemon peel and juice, and add the margarine. Continue stirring. Add food coloring and stir until blended. Fill pie crust, tarts or use as a lemon custard.

For **Lemon Meringue Pie**: Pour filling in baked crust, top with meringue and brown under broiler (about five minutes).

Meringue

3 EGG WHITES
1 Tbsp. SUGAR
1/4 tsp. CREAM OF TARTAR

Beat ingredients together until stiff then layer over filling.

Per serving

Calories	111	Saturated Fat	0.2 gm
Cholesterol	0	Sodium	94.5 mg

Low-Calorie Apple Pie

♥ Yield: 6 to 8 servings

7 lg. green APPLES
1/2 cup BROWN SUGAR
1 Tbsp. CINNAMON
1 Tbsp. NUTMEG
1/2 tsp. ground GINGER
2 Tbsp. CORNSTARCH
1 Tbsp. LEMON JUICE
1 9" double PIE CRUST
1 Tbsp. SKIM MILK

Preheat oven to 450 F. Peel, core and slice apples thin and place in a large bowl. Add in next six ingredients. Mix well.

Pour into unbaked 9" pie shell, mounding higher in the center. Cover with top crust. Crimp edges, so juices will not escape, and make slits on top with sharp knife for steam. Brush top with milk, cover edges with foil and bake at 450 F for 15 minutes, then reduce heat to 425 F. Bake 35 minutes more (or until pie is bubbling).

Note: Keep pie dough refrigerated until needed.

Per serving

Calories .... 143.7   Saturated Fat 0
Cholesterol 0   Sodium .... 42.8 mg

Oat Bran Crumb Apple Pie
(no crust)

♥ Yield: 6 servings

6 baking APPLES (peeled, cored and sliced thin)
2 Tbsp. LEMON JUICE
1 Tbsp. CINNAMON
1 tsp. NUTMEG
1 tsp. GINGER
1/4 cup BROWN SUGAR
3 Tbsp. diet MARGARINE (melted)
1 cup OAT BRAN
1/4 cup BROWN SUGAR

Preheat oven to 400 F. In a medium-size bowl, mix together first six ingredients. Coat and turn apples with ingredients, mixing thoroughly.

Pour into 9" pie pan. Top with one tablespoon margarine, drizzling here and there.

In a small bowl, mix oat bran and two tablespoons of melted margarine. Add the quarter-cup brown sugar and mix with fork. Distribute over apple mixture evenly.

Bake at 400 F for 45 minutes. Serve warm or cold.

Note: Serve with non-fat frozen yogurt.

Per serving

Calories 239.6	Saturated Fat .....0.6 gm
Cholesterol 0	Sodium ....75 mg

Cranberry-Cherry Pie

♥ Yield: 8 to 10 servings

1 can (21 oz.) CHERRY PIE FILLING
1 can (16 oz.) whole CRANBERRY SAUCE
2 pkgs. (1/2 oz. each) SUGAR SUBSTITUTE
3 Tbsp. quick-cooking TAPIOCA
1 tsp. LEMON JUICE
1/4 tsp. CINNAMON
2 Tbsp. diet MARGARINE
1/2 cup BREAD CRUMBS
1 10" double PIE CRUST
2 tsp. BREAD CRUMBS
1 Tbsp. SKIM MILK

Preheat oven to 400 F. In a large bowl, combine first eight ingredients. Mix well. Sprinkle bread crumbs on bottom of 10" pie crust and pour in filling. Top with rolled top crust. Arrange in a design or lattice to escape steam.

Brush top with milk and bake at 400 F for 30 minutes (or until pie is browned and bubbly). To avoid scorching, cover edge with foil. If pie has not browned enough, bake 15 minutes more.

Note: Keep pie dough refrigerated until needed.

Per serving

Calories 241	Saturated Fat .....0.6 gm
Cholesterol ....0.5 mg	Sodium ....149 mg

Sweet Potato Pecan Pie

♥ Yield: 8 servings

Part I

1 pkg. (4 oz.) EGG SUBSTITUTE (found in dairy section)
1/2 cup BROWN SUGAR SUBSTITUTE
1 Tbsp. diet MARGARINE (melted)
1 Tbsp. VANILLA EXTRACT
1 1/2 Tbsp. MAPLE SYRUP
1 cup whole PECANS
1 single PIE CRUST (unbaked)*

Preheat oven to 350 F. Add all ingredients (except pie crust) in medium-size bowl. Mix thoroughly and pour into unbaked 9" or 10" pie shell. Pie shell should not be pierced. Bake 30 minutes at 350 F. Set aside for filling.

*See pie crust recipes on pages 88 and 89.

Part II

3 lg. SWEET POTATOES (peeled, boiled and mashed)
1/4 tsp. GINGER
1/4 tsp. CINNAMON
1/4 tsp. CLOVES
1 EGG WHITE (beaten with 1 tsp. SUGAR)

Add all ingredients in medium-size bowl. Mix well and pour over prebaked pecan mixture above. Return to oven and bake at 350 F for 25 minutes more.

Per serving

Calories 262	Saturated Fat .....1.4 gm
Cholesterol ....0.1 mg	Sodium ....109 mg

Old-Fashioned Pumpkin Pie

♥ Yield: 8 servings

1/2 pkg. (4 oz.) EGG SUBSTITUTE (or 3 egg whites)
2 1/2 Tbsp. FRUCTOSE
3/4 tsp. CINNAMON
1 1/2 tsp. PUMPKIN PIE SPICE
1 can (16 oz.) cooked PUMPKIN
    (unsalted, if possible)
1/3 cup unsweetened
    ORANGE JUICE
3/4 cup evaporated non-fat MILK
2 EGG WHITES
1/4 tsp. CREAM OF TARTAR
1 single PIE CRUST (unbaked)*

Preheat oven to 350 F. In medium-size bowl, combine first seven ingredients. Mix thoroughly. In separate bowl, beat egg whites with cream of tartar until stiff. Fold into pumpkin mixture folding over four times.

Pour into 10" unbaked pie crust. Bake at 350 F for 60 to 65 minutes, or until inserted knife comes out clean.

*See pie crust recipes on pages 88 and 89.

Per serving

Calories 148	Saturated Fat ..... 0.6 gm
Cholesterol .... 0.9 mg	Sodium .... 264 mg

Easy Pumpkin Pie

♥ Yield: 6 servings

1 cup ANIMAL CRACKERS
1 Tbsp. CANOLA OIL
1 Tbsp. diet MARGARINE (melted)
2 cups PUMPKIN (cooked)
2 Tbsp. FRUCTOSE
**3/4 pkg. (4 oz.) EGG SUBSTITUTE (found in dairy
    section)**
1 tsp. CINNAMON
1 tsp. PUMPKIN SPICE
1/2 tsp. CLOVES
3/4 cup SKIM MILK

Preheat oven to 425 F. In a blender, whiz animal crackers to crumbs. Combine in a small bowl, animal cracker crumbs, oil and melted margarine. With back of tablespoon, press mixture halfway up the sides of a 9" pie pan. Bake at 425 F for 10 minutes. Set aside.

In a blender, puree cooked pumpkin. Combine in medium-size bowl two cups pureed pumpkin and rest of ingredients. Mix thoroughly.

Pour into baked cracker shell. Return to oven and bake at 350 F for 45 to 50 minutes. Serve cold with whipped evaporated skim milk or topping of choice.

Per serving

Calories 210	Saturated Fat ..... 1.7 gm
Cholesterol .... 7.9 mg	Sodium .... 64.0 mg

Strawberries & Raspberries in Meringue Baskets

♥ Yield: 6 to 8 baskets

8 EGG WHITES
1/2 tsp. CREAM OF TARTAR
2 cups SUGAR
2 cups STRAWBERRIES (cleaned and hulled)
2 cups RASPBERRIES (cleaned)

Preheat oven to 200 F. Combine first three ingredients in electric mixer and beat on high until stiff and shiny. Scoop into pastry bag with star tip. Line 18" baking sheet with parchment paper and draw eight four-inch circles. Pipe a layer of meringue to completely cover circle outline and continue piping smaller circles inside the large outline, forming a disk. Bake at 200 F for 30 minutes.

On second baking sheet also lined with parchment, draw as many four-inch circles as can fit. Pipe a layer of meringue on the outline of each circle. (You will need 24 circles.) Bake at 200 F for 30 minutes.

Pipe a meringue circle on the outer edge of the disks. Place one of the circles on top. Repeat, piping meringue circles and placing baked circles on top. Your basket should have a bottom disk with three rings on top. To form a strong bond, pipe stars up and down sides of basket. Place on baking sheet lined with parchment paper and return to oven to bake at 200 F for 30 minutes more. Fill with berries and serve.

Per serving

Calories 235	Saturated Fat 0
Cholesterol 0	Sodium ....51.0 mg

Strawberry Tarts

♥ Yield: 12 tarts

2 1/4 cups all-purpose FLOUR
2 Tbsp. SUGAR
1 soft tub (8 oz.) MARGARINE
1 EGG
1 tsp. VANILLA EXTRACT
4 Tbsp. ICE WATER (more if needed)

Preheat oven to 400 F. Combine all ingredients in food processor. Mix just enough to bring dough to a ball. Remove dough and place on flour-sprinkled working surface.

Cut into 12 pieces and roll each piece into a five-inch circle. Fit into muffin or tart tins. Bake at 400 F for 12 minutes. Tarts should be lightly browned.

Filling

1 pkg. (8 oz.) instant VANILLA PUDDING
1 1/2 cups cold SKIM MILK
2 sm. baskets STRAWBERRIES (cleaned and hulled)

In medium-size bowl, mix pudding with cold milk. Beat slowly with electric hand beater, until consistency of whipped cream. Spoon even amount into tart shells. Top with strawberries.

Glaze

1/2 cup light CORN SYRUP
1/2 Tbsp. WATER

In small pan, boil syrup and water. Dip pastry brush in syrup and glaze strawberries.

Per serving

Calories 179.7	Saturated Fat ..... 1.0 gm
Cholesterol 0	Sodium .... 132.5 mg

Easy Peach Turnovers

♥ Yield: about 48 turnovers

PIE CRUST DOUGH*
12 PEACHES (slightly ripe, peeled and sliced thin)
3/4 cup BROWN SUGAR
2 Tbsp. ARROWROOT (found in health food stores)
2 Tbsp. CINNAMON
1 Tbsp. NUTMEG
1/2 tsp. GINGER
2 Tbsp. LEMON JUICE

Preheat oven to 425 F. Prepare pie crust dough (*see crust recipes on pages 88 and 89). Cover and refrigerate. Mix next seven ingredients thoroughly in a medium-size bowl. Set aside.

Remove cool dough from refrigerator and roll on flour-sprinkled working area. Roll pieces of dough into six-inch rounds. Place two tablespoons of peach mixture in center of each and fold over into half moons. Wet edges with water and press with fork tines to seal.

Set 12 turnovers at a time on a 9" x 13" baking sheet and bake at 425 F for 15 minutes. Reduce heat to 350 F and continue baking for 30 minutes more.

While still warm, sprinkle turnovers with cinnamon mixed with sugar.

Each turnover

Calories 36.2		Saturated Fat ...0.07 gm	
Cholesterol 0		Sodium ....12.2 mg	

Walnut Cloud Cookies

♥ Yield: 36 cookies

3 EGG WHITES
1/2 tsp. CREAM OF TARTAR
2/3 cup SUGAR
1/2 tsp. VANILLA EXTRACT
3/4 cup WALNUTS (chopped)
3 Tbsp. COCOA
Non-stick COOKING SPRAY (to spray cookie sheet)

Preheat oven to 200 F. With electric mixer, beat egg whites and cream of tartar on high until glossy. Add sugar and vanilla extract. Beat in thoroughly. Fold in walnuts and cocoa.

Drop heaping teaspoonfuls onto sprayed 10" x 18" cookie sheet, one inch apart. Bake at 200 F for 60 minutes. Outside should be dry. Store in airtight container.

Each cookie

Calories 32.9	Saturated Fat ..... 0.1 gm
Cholesterol 0	Sodium .... 4.8 mg

Banana-Oatmeal Cookies
(low-calorie)

♥ Yield: about 24 cookies

1 3/4 cups FLOUR
1 1/2 cups ROLLED OATS (quick cooking)
1 tsp. BAKING SODA
1 tsp. BAKING POWDER
1/2 cup BROWN SUGAR SUBSTITUTE (found in health
    food stores)
1/2 tsp. CINNAMON
1 tsp. LECITHIN granules (found in health food stores)
1/4 cup CANOLA OIL
1/2 cup plain non-fat YOGURT
1/2 tsp. LEMON JUICE
2 ripe BANANAS
1/2 cup WALNUTS (chopped)
2 Tbsp. APPLE JUICE
Non-stick COOKING SPRAY (to spray baking sheets)

Preheat oven to 350 F. In an electric mixer, add ingredients in order given. Mix on low until all ingredients are incorporated. Drop by tablespoons on sprayed 10" x 18" cookie sheets. Press batter (with bottom of drinking glass) as you drop it on cookie tray, making cookies uniform.

Bake at 350 F for 25 minutes. Cookies puff up and have a cake-like texture.

Each cookie

Calories	91	Saturated Fat	0.4 gm
Cholesterol	0.08 mg	Sodium	31.6 mg

Cocoa-Oatmeal Cookies

♥ Yield: 36 cookies

1 1/2 cups ROLLED OATS
2/3 cup all-purpose FLOUR
1/4 cup unsweetened COCOA
1/2 tsp. BAKING SODA
1/2 tsp. BAKING POWDER
12 Tbsp. diet MARGARINE (unsalted)
1 cup BROWN SUGAR SUBSTITUTE (found in
     health food stores)
2 EGG WHITES
1 1/2 tsp. VANILLA EXTRACT
1/2 cup plain non-fat YOGURT
1 cup WALNUTS (chopped)
1/2 cup RAISINS
Non-stick COOKING SPRAY (to spray cookie sheet)

Preheat oven to 350 F. In a large bowl, mix first five ingredients. In another bowl (medium), beat together margarine and sugar substitute for one minute. Add egg whites, vanilla and yogurt. Beat to a creamy texture. Fold in walnuts and raisins. Mix and add to dry ingredients. Mix until all ingredients are thoroughly absorbed. Drop from heaping tea-spoons onto sprayed 10" x 18" cookie sheet, one inch apart.

Bake at 350 F for 20 minutes. Cookies will have a cake-like texture and are delicious.

Each cookie

Calories	64	Saturated Fat	0.7 gm
Cholesterol	0.05 mg	Sodium	60.5 mg

Royal Oatmeal Cookies

♥ Yield: 36 cookies

1/2 cup CANOLA OIL
1/2 cup BROWN SUGAR SUBSTITUTE (found in
  health food stores)
2 Tbsp. GRANULATED SUGAR
1 EGG WHITE (beaten frothy)
3/4 tsp. VANILLA EXTRACT
3 Tbsp. WATER
2 cups ROLLED OATS
1/3 cup white PASTRY FLOUR
1/3 cup whole wheat PASTRY FLOUR
1/4 tsp. BAKING SODA
1/4 tsp. BAKING POWDER
1 tsp. CINNAMON
1/2 cup WALNUTS (chopped)

Preheat oven to 350 F. In medium-size bowl, cream together oil and sugars. Add beaten egg white, vanilla, water and rolled oats. Add rest of dry ingredients as listed and mix for one minute. Do not overmix.

Dip teaspoon in water and drop a heaping teaspoonful of batter two inches apart on 10" x 18" cookie sheet, lined with parchment paper. Press down with back of spoon and bake at 350 F for 13 - 15 minutes.

Each cookie

Calories	55	Saturated Fat	0.3 gm
Cholesterol	0	Sodium	64 mg

Momma Stefana's
Italian Cookies

♥ Yield: about 60 cookies

3 1/2 cups sifted all-purpose FLOUR
4 tsp. BAKING POWDER
4 tsp. SUGAR SUBSTITUTE
8 oz. soft MARGARINE (in tub)
7 EGG WHITES
1 tsp. VANILLA EXTRACT
12 drops ANISE OIL (not extract)
GLAZED FRUIT and/or ALMONDS for decorating

Preheat oven to 375 F. Sift together flour and baking powder. Set aside. With an electric mixer, beat together sugar substitute and margarine until fluffy. Beat in eggs and add flavorings.

Add dry ingredients gradually, beating on low. Continue until batter is almost like pie dough. If too soft, add a little more flour. Gather into a ball, cover and refrigerate for one hour.

Fill a cookie gun and drop on ungreased 10" x 18" cookie sheet, one inch apart. Add glazed fruit or almond in center of cookies and bake at 375 F for 15 to 20 minutes (or until lightly browned).

(Author's note: This recipe is dedicated to my mother, who dictated the ingredients to me.)

Each cookie

Calories	44.6	Saturated Fat	0.3 gm
Cholesterol	0	Sodium	64.6 mg

Swedish Cookies

♥ Yield: about 100 cookies

1 cup MARGARINE (soft tub)
1 1/4 cups SUGAR
2 EGG WHITES
1 Tbsp. GRAND MARNIER
2 Tbsp. MOLASSES
1 Tbsp. WATER
1 tsp. LEMON PEEL
1 tsp. CINNAMON
1 tsp. GINGER
1 tsp. NUTMEG
4 1/2 cups all-purpose FLOUR
1 tsp. BAKING SODA
1 Tbsp. BAKING POWDER
ICING (or sprinkles) to decorate
Non-stick COOKING SPRAY (to spray cookie sheet)

Preheat oven to 375 F. In a large bowl, mix together margarine, sugar and egg whites, beating until fluffy. Add in Grand Marnier, molasses, water, lemon peel and spices. While beating, gradually add flour, baking soda and baking powder. Beat well.

Refrigerate for two hours. When ready, roll out small squares one-quarter-inch thick on pastry cloth and cut with desired cutters. Place on 10" x 18" sprayed cookie sheet one inch apart and bake for eight minutes at 375 F. Cool and decorate or frost. Perfect for Christmas cookies!

Each cookie

Calories 39.5	Saturated Fat .....0.1 gm
Cholesterol 0	Sodium ....36.1 mg

Thumbelina Cookies

♥ Yield: about 50 cookies

1/4 cup diet MARGARINE
1/3 cup BROWN SUGAR
1/2 cup GRANULATED SUGAR
2 EGG WHITES (beaten frothy)
1/2 tsp. ALMOND EXTRACT
1 3/4 cups sifted all-purpose FLOUR
1/2 tsp. BAKING POWDER
1/8 tsp. BAKING SODA
1/4 cup low calorie STRAWBERRY JAM
Non-stick COOKING SPRAY (to spray cookie sheet)

Preheat oven to 350 F. With electric mixer, cream margarine and sugars. Add egg whites and almond extract, and continue beating on high. Add flour, baking powder and soda. Mix thoroughly and refrigerate for 30 minutes.

When ready, shape into balls, using one teaspoonful per cookie. Place two inches apart on sprayed 10" x 18" cookie sheet and press centers with thumb. Place one-quarter teaspoonful of strawberry jam in pressed centers and bake at 350 F for eight minutes.

Note: This is another low-calorie, low-fat treat.

Each cookie

Calories 36   Saturated Fat ... 0.09 gm
Cholesterol 0   Sodium .... 17.8 mg

Low-Calorie Brownies

♥ Yield: 10 to 12 servings

1/4 cup diet MARGARINE
1/4 cup unsweetened COCOA
1 pkg. (4 oz.) EGG SUBSTITUTE (in dairy section)
1/3 cup FRUCTOSE
1 tsp. VANILLA EXTRACT
1/3 cup all-purpose FLOUR
1/2 tsp. BAKING POWDER
1/2 cup WALNUTS (chopped)
Non-stick COOKING SPRAY (to spray baking pan)

Preheat oven to 350 F. In a small pan over low heat, melt margarine with cocoa. Set aside.

In electric mixer bowl, add egg substitute, fructose and vanilla. Beat on low for one minute and add cocoa mixture. Mix well and slowly add flour and baking powder. Beat for two minutes on high. Fold in walnuts.

Pour into sprayed 8" square pan and bake at 350 F for 20 minutes. Cool and cut into squares.

Per serving

Calories 94	Saturated Fat .....0.5 gm
Cholesterol 0	Sodium ....59.5 mg

Country Brownies

♥ Yield: 9 brownies

1/3 cup CANOLA OIL
1/4 cup SUGAR
2 EGGS (or 4 egg whites)
2 tsp. VANILLA EXTRACT
1/4 cup unsifted all-purpose FLOUR
1/3 cup COCOA
1/2 tsp. BAKING POWDER
1 cup WALNUTS (chopped)
Non-stick COOKING SPRAY (to spray cake pan)

Preheat oven to 350 F. In electric mixer (or medium-size bowl), beat together oil, sugar, eggs and vanilla. Add flour, cocoa and baking powder. Stir or beat until well-blended and creamy. Set aside two tablespoons walnuts and fold remainder into batter. Fold over 10 times.

Spoon batter on sprayed 8" square cake pan and bake at 350 F for 20 minutes. While still warm, glaze with chocolate icing (optional).

Chocolate Icing

1/2 cup POWDERED SUGAR
2 Tbsp. COCOA
2 to 3 Tbsp. MILK

Mix together all ingredients thoroughly and spread on brownies. Top with two tablespoons of walnuts.

Each Serving

Calories 232	Saturated Fat .....2.0 gm
Cholesterol ....0.09 mg	Sodium ....46.7 mg

Banana Cream Cups

♥ Yield: 4 servings

1 pkg. (1 oz.) sugar-free BANANA PUDDING
2 cups SKIM MILK
1/4 tsp. MACE
2 lg. BANANAS
1 tsp. CINNAMON
1/2 cup WALNUTS (grated)

Prepare pudding according to directions on package, using skim milk and add mace. Cut bananas in half, use one-half for each serving.

Spoon into pudding cups one layer of pudding and one layer of sliced bananas. Build two layers, ending with the pudding. (Sprinkle each pudding cup with cinnamon and one tablespoon of walnuts.) Place in freezer for 10 minutes and serve.

Each Serving

Calories .... 105.5   Saturated Fat ..... 1.1 gm
Cholesterol .... 3.0 mg   Sodium .... 85.2 mg

Baked Apples

♥ Yield: 2 servings

2 lg. DELICIOUS APPLES
1 slice homemade (or other) BREAD
1/2 tsp. CINNAMON
1 tsp. BROWN SUGAR
1/4 tsp. LEMON EXTRACT
2 Tbsp. WATER

Core apples almost to bottom. Leave a little skin at bottom, so apples will remain firm. Toast slice of bread and whiz in blender for bread crumbs. Mix crumbs with cinnamon, sugar and lemon extract. Stuff cored apples with crumb mixture and place in microwave pan. Add water, cover with plastic wrap and microwave on high for four minutes. Place in freezer for five minutes and serve.

Note: If microwave oven is not available, steam in oven for 30 minutes uncovered.

Each Serving

Calories 146.5	Saturated Fat 0
Cholesterol 0	Sodium .... 1.6 mg

Gelatin Parfaits

♥ Yield: 4 servings

1 pkg. (6 oz.) sugar-free raspberry JELL-O®
2 cups hot WATER
1 pkg. (1 oz.) sugar-free VANILLA PUDDING
2 cups SKIM MILK
1 jar (3 oz.) MARASCHINO CHERRIES (and juice)

Prepare Jello-O according to directions on package using the two cups hot water. Refrigerate until jelled.

Prepare pudding using the two cups milk, according to directions on package. Chill.

Using four parfait glasses, spoon in gelatin and pudding, alternating and smoothing each layer with back of spoon. Top each serving with a maraschino cherry and some of the juice.

Note: Use any flavor pudding for taste variations.

Each Serving

Calories ....83.5   Saturated Fat .....0.1 gm
Cholesterol 0   Sodium ....383 mg

Special-Treat Strawberries

♥ Yield: 5 servings

1 cup SUGAR
3/4 cup WATER
10 extra-large, firm STRAWBERRIES (with long stems)

In quart pan, dissolve sugar in water, cooking and stirring until mixture begins to boil. Insert candy thermometer in sugar mixture and when syrup reaches 300 F remove pan from heat.

Have strawberries ready, and working very quickly, dip strawberries in syrup, holding by stems or using dipping fork. Syrup is very hot! Let excess syrup drip off and place berries on 10" x 13" cookie tray. Let glaze harden. Serve within one or two hours.

Each Serving

Calories 172	Saturated Fat .....0.1 gm
Cholesterol 0	Sodium ....0.8 mg

Ice Cream Deluxe

♥ Yield: 2 servings

**2 cups frozen non-fat
      YOGURT (any flavor)
2 Tbsp. crushed
      PINEAPPLE
1 Tbsp. WALNUTS (chopped)**

Divide yogurt into two dessert cups. Add one tablespoon of crushed pineapple and a little of the juice to each serving. Top each with chopped walnuts.

Each Serving

Calories 138	Saturated Fat ..... 0.3 gm
Cholesterol .... 4.0 mg	Sodium .... 174.1 mg

Super Sundae

♥ Yield: 1 serving

1 cup STRAWBERRIES
1 pkg. (1/2 oz.) GELATIN (can be flavored)
1 cup non-fat YOGURT (any flavor)
Sprinkle of SUGAR

Clean and stem strawberries and puree in blender. Pour into medium-size bowl, reserving one table-spoon puree. Add gelatin. Mix well and set in refrigerator until slightly thickened.

Take out and add yogurt and sprinkle of sugar. Return to refrigerator until texture is firm (as of soft ice cream). Spoon into ice cream dish and garnish with reserved puree.

Note: Other fruit, such as peaches, raspberries, blackberries or ripe cantaloupe can be used.

Each Serving

Calories 195	Saturated Fat ..... 0.3 gm
Cholesterol 0	Sodium .... 176 mg

Substitutions

Margarine, shortening, butter or solid fat products:

For one-third cup margarine, shortening or butter—two tablespoons oil

For one-half stick margarine or solid fat product—six tablespoons oil

Baking Chocolate:

Use three tablespoons cocoa plus one tablespoon oil for one square baking chocolate.

Sweeteners:

Sugar substitute can be used in cooking, however, read the directions to see if the product can be used to cook with. Corn syrup and applesauce help reduce the amount of sugar called for in recipes.

Fat Free Buttermilk Substitute:

To one-half cup strained fresh buttermilk add three cups skim milk. Place in refrigerator overnight to curdle.

Eggs:

For one egg yolk, beat one egg white, add one-quarter teaspoon lecithin granules, and one and one-half teaspoons oil. For one whole egg, beat two egg whites, add one-quarter teaspoon lecithin granules, and one and one-half teaspoons oil. To reconstitute egg white powder, use one tablespoon powder, add two tablespoons warm water and beat at high speed. Use in place of egg whites.

Low Calorie Cream Cheese:

Two cups plain low-fat yogurt, place in double-layer cheesecloth, twist and tie with string. Hang overnight over sink to drain, or place in colander-lined container in refrigerator. Let drip 12 to 14 hours.

Mock Sour Cream:

One cup low-fat cottage cheese, one tablespoon lemon juice and two tablespoons skim milk. Mix in blender until smooth. Yield: 1 1/4 cups.

Protein Spread:

One-quarter cup non-fat dry milk, add one-half cup no-oil peanut butter. Mix thoroughly. A good spread on bread, buns or muffins.

Flavorful Salt Substitutes

For Cooked Foods

3 tsp. BASIL
2 tsp. SAVORY HERBS
2 tsp. CELERY SEED
2 tsp. ground CUMIN
2 tsp. SAGE
1/2 tsp. each, black, red, white, green PEPPERCORNS
1 tsp. THYME
1 tsp. ROSEMARY
2 tsp. MARJORAM

Mix ingredients thoroughly in blender. Store in glass container. Good for cooked stews, soups, broiled and baked foods.

For Salads and Uncooked Foods

2 tsp. GARLIC POWDER
1 tsp. BASIL
1 tsp. ANISE SEED
1 tsp. OREGANO
1/2 tsp. each, black, white, green PEPPERCORNS
   (available in market herb section)
1 tsp. ROSEMARY
1 tsp. granulated LEMON RIND

Mix ingredients thoroughly in blender. Store in a glass jar. Good for salads and uncooked foods.

Sodium Information

One teaspoon salt has 2300 milligrams sodium
One teaspoon baking soda has 1000 milligrams sodium
One teaspoon monosodium glutamate has 750 milligrams sodium
One teaspoon baking powder has 329 milligrams sodium
Sodium Free—less than five milligrams of sodium per serving
Low Sodium—140 milligrams or less of sodium per serving
Very Low Sodium—less than 35 milligrams of sodium per serving

Sample Menus

(Before changing your diet, consult your doctor.)

The following sample menus are a guide for a healthy eating pattern.

Breakfast: (1) Fruit (2) Cereal (3) Toast/Jam (4) Beverage
Changes on (2) can be made to fit the morning mood.

Lunch: (1) Small Fruit (2) Tuna Salad (3) Beverage
Again, (2) can be changed accordingly.

Dinner: (1) Salad (2) Entree (3) Two Vegetables (4) Jello-O®
(5) Beverage. Occasionally, a cookie or sweet treat. As
with breakfast and lunch, (2) can be changed to fit the day.

An easy-to-remember code for vegetables is A,B,C—A-Asparagus, B-Broccoli, and C-Cauliflower. Of course, other vegetables can be substituted, but if we computerize our brain to guide us, then we can react accordingly.

Sensible portions of all foods we eat makes our living pattern easier. And—let us not forget to drink plenty of water.

If that irresistible urge pops up for an evening snack, indulge in air-popped popcorn. A scrumptious treat.

Breakfast Plan

A. 1 1/4 cups Cheerios®
1/2 cup SKIM MILK
1 sm. BANANA, sliced
BEVERAGE

B. 1/2 GRAPEFRUIT
1/2 cup OATMEAL
1/2 cup SKIM MILK
1/2 tsp. CINNAMON (sprinkle on oatmeal)
BEVERAGE

C. 1/2 cup mixed FRUIT
VEGETABLE OMELET
2 slices TOAST (homemade bread)
BEVERAGE

D. 1/2 CANTALOUPE
1 cup PUFFED CORN
1/2 cup SKIM MILK
BEVERAGE

E. 1 GRAPEFRUIT juice (small)
1/2 cup cooked OAT BRAN
2 slices TOAST (homemade bread)
BEVERAGE

Lunch Plan

A. Fruit Plate Salad
1/4 CANTALOUPE (cubed)
1/2 BANANA (sliced)
1/2 cup STRAWBERRIES
1 Tbsp. RAISINS
4 Tbsp. non-fat YOGURT
Arrange on LETTUCE and serve with CRISP CRACKERS.

B. Large Mixed Salad
1 cup shredded LETTUCE
1 CUCUMBER, sliced
1 TOMATO, sliced
1/4 ONION, sliced
raw ZUCCHINI
1/2 GRAPEFRUIT in sections
Arrange on platter, drizzle with any low-calorie dressing.
Serve with CRACKERS.

C. Hot Vegetable Plate
1/2 cup BROCCOLI flowerettes
1/2 cup summer SQUASH (quartered)
1/2 cup BEETS (sliced)
Arrange on platter, add two tablespoons water. Cover with plastic wrap and microwave on medium high for 10 minutes. Serve with 1/4 cup COTTAGE CHEESE and 1/2 cup YOGURT with added FRUIT of choice.

D. Tuna Fish Salad Plate
1 1/2 oz. TUNA (in spring water)
1 sm. APPLE (cubed)
1/2 Tbsp. ONION (chopped)

1 stalk CELERY (chopped)
1 Tbsp. diet MAYONNAISE
1 tsp. dry MUSTARD

Mix all ingredients and arrange on bed of LETTUCE. Slice one medium TOMATO in rounds and serve with CRISP CRACKER.

E. Asparagus Quiche (see page 28)
Follow recipe. Serve with TOAST. All selections should include BEVERAGE of choice.

Dinner Plan

A. FILLED TURKEY ROLLS (see page 52)
SALAD
2 VEGETABLES (1/2 cup each)
Low-cal JELL-0® (1/2 cup)
BEVERAGE

B. POACHED SALMON (see page 64)
STEAMED CARROTS (1/2 cup)
TOMATOES and CUCUMBERS, sliced
Low-cal PUDDING (1/2 cup)
BEVERAGE

C. SPAGHETTI & TURKEY MEATBALLS with TOMATO SAUCE
(see page 54)
GREEN SALAD (with VINEGAR-OIL dressing)
Low-cal JELL-0® (1/2 cup)
BEVERAGE

D. INDIVIDUAL SPINACH POCKETS (see page 36)
THREE-BEAN SALAD (1 cup) (see page 17)
HEALTHY CARROT CAKE (1 slice) (see page 81)
BEVERAGE

E. Choice of any Entree
FROZEN DESSERT
BEVERAGE

Glossary

Saturated Fats:

Generally solid at room temperature. Foods high in saturated fats are: red meats, whole milk, dairy products, butter and cheese. Saturated vegetable fats are: coconut oil, palm oil, palm kernel oil, and hydrogenated vegetable oils. Hydrogenated fats such as shortening and margarine are polyunsaturated liquid oils which have been chemically-converted into saturated fats at room temperatures. Coconut oil, palm and palm kernel oils are highly-saturated fats found in a majority of baked items.

Monounsaturated Fats:

The richest source of monounsaturated fat is olive oil. There is some scientific evidence that monounsaturated fats help in lowering the bad cholesterol without also lowering the good cholesterol. I use olive and canola oils in cooking and salad dressings.

Polyunsaturated Fats:

Polyunsaturated fats are generally liquid at room temperature. Vegetable oils, except coconut and palm oils, are high in polyunsaturated fat.

Cholesterol:

A waxy substance related to fats, which is present in foods of animal origin. Some is manufactured by the body. It has an important role in food digestion, production of some hormones, and in providing insulation for the nervous system. It is a fatty substance that is carried through the blood. Since the fatty substance cannot be dissolved in the blood, the body takes care of them in its own way, and makes what we understand it to be bad and good cholesterol. To help eliminate bad cholesterol, doctors recommend low-fat diets, and to help the good cholesterol, healthy no-fat eating and exercise.

Triglycerides:

Type of fat (carried in the blood) manufactured by the body from excess calories. Fats we do not use for energy are stored as triglycerides. Doctors recommend blood test periodically to monitor the count. This type of test is simple and inexpensive, done just by pricking a finger. Eating too much sugar contributes to high counts. Remember to exercise at your level.

Index

Meet the Author

Teacher, lecturer and authority on the subject of cooking for a healthy heart, Virginia Defendorf developed her culinary skills through contact with ethnic groups and extensive travel.

Mrs. Defendorf is the author of *"Let's Learn Cake Artistry,"* *"Let's Learn Baking"* and *"Let's Learn Gourmet Cooking"* which she prepared for vocational education in San Juan Capistrano schools.

In preparation for **Recipes for a Healthy Lifestyle** she concentrated on creating recipes that are appetizing yet healthful. Her goal was to develop a diet that would ensure that her husband's arteries remained unclogged following quadruple bypass surgery.

She worked closely with her husband's personal physician and the Scripps Cardiac Institute, who periodically monitored Mr. Defendorf's cholesterol range.

Virginia, a native of Michigan, attended Marygrove College in Detroit and the University of California Long Beach. She holds a degree in home economics and has taught for more than three decades.

She is a professional baker and is frequently called upon to judge cooking contests. Virginia and her husband, Edward, reside in San Juan Capistrano, California, when they are not visiting their children in various parts of the country.

Because of her understanding of ethnic foods and spices, she was able to combine various foods and herbs to fit the American palate. Teaching students to cook has helped her acquire the ability to write recipes that are easy to follow. These skills were combined to produce **Recipes for a Healthy Lifestyle.**

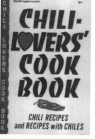

SALSA LOVERS COOK BOOK

More than 180 taste-tempting recipes for salsas that will make every meal a special event! Salsas for salads, appetizers, main dishes and desserts! Put some salsa in your life! By Susan K. Bollin.

5 1/2 x 8 1/2 — 128 pages . . . $5.95

CHIP & DIP LOVERS COOK BOOK

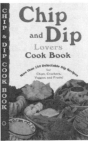

More than 150 recipes for fun and festive dips. Make southwestern dips, dips with fruits and vegetables, meats, poultry and seafood. Salsa dips and dips for desserts. Includes recipes for making homemade chips. By Susan K. Bollin.

5 1/2 x 8 1/2 — 112 pages . . . $5.95

QUICK-N-EASY MEXICAN RECIPES

More than 175 favorite Mexican recipes you can prepare in less than thirty minutes. Traditional items such as tacos, tostadas and enchiladas. Also features easy recipes for salads, soups, breads, desserts and drinks. By Susan K. Bollin.

5 1/2 x 8 1/2 — 128 pages . . . $5.95

WHOLLY FRIJOLES!
The Whole Bean Cook Book

Features a wide variety of recipes for salads, main dishes, side dishes and desserts with an emphasis on Southwestern style. Pinto, kidney, garbanzo, black, red and navy beans, you'll find recipes for these and many more! Includes cooking tips and fascinating bean trivia! By Shayne Fischer.

5 1/2 x 8 1/2—112 pages . . . $6.95

TORTILLA LOVERS COOK BOOK

From tacos to tostadas, enchiladas to nachos, every dish celebrates the tortilla! More than 100 easy to prepare, festive recipes for breakfast, lunch and dinner. Filled with Southwestern flavors! By Bruce and Bobbi Fischer.

5 1/2 x 8 1/2 — 112 pages . . . $6.95

ORDER BLANK

GOLDEN WEST PUBLISHERS

☼ 4113 N. Longview Ave. • Phoenix, AZ 85014

602-265-4392 • **1-800-658-5830** • FAX 602-279-6901

Qty	Title	Price	Amount
	Apple Lovers Cook Book	6.95	
	Best Barbecue Recipes	5.95	
	Chili-Lovers' Cook Book	5.95	
	Chip and Dip Lovers Cook Book	5.95	
	Citrus Lovers Cook Book	6.95	
	Date Recipes	6.95	
	Easy Recipes for Wild Game & Fish	6.95	
	Joy of Muffins	5.95	
	Low Fat Mexican Recipes	6.95	
	Mexican Desserts & Drinks	6.95	
	Mexican Family Favorites Cook Book	6.95	
	Pecan Lovers Cook Book	6.95	
	Pumpkin Lovers Cook Book	6.95	
	Quick Bread Cook Book	6.95	
	Quick-n-Easy Mexican Recipes	5.95	
	Recipes for a Healthy Lifestyle	6.95	
	Salsa Lovers Cook Book	5.95	
	Veggie Lovers Cook Book	6.95	
	Vegi-Mex (Vegetarian Mexican Recipes)	6.95	
	Wholly Frijoles! The Whole Bean Cook Book	6.95	

| Shipping & Handling Add ➠ | U.S. & Canada | $3.00 | |
| | Other countries | $5.00 | |

☐ My Check or Money Order Enclosed $

☐ MasterCard   ☐ VISA ($20 credit card minimum)

(Payable in U.S. funds)

Acct. No.   Exp. Date

Signature

Name   Telephone

Address

City/State/Zip

9/98   **Call for FREE catalog**   Recipes for a Healthy Lifestyle

This order blank may be photo-copied.